MUSIC, FRIENDS and PLACES

A Memoir

Howard Ferguson

Thames Publishing
London

First published in 1997 by Thames Publishing
14 Barlby Road, London W10 6AR

Text copyright @ 1997 Howard Ferguson

No part of this publication may be reproduced in any form (photographic, mechanical, electronic), or for any purpose. without the prior written permission of the publisher.

Printed and bound in Great Britain
by Lonsdale Press Ltd.

Contents

Chapter One: Beginnings, 1908-1925 7
    Interlude I: Harold Samuel (1879-1937) 16
Chapter Two: 12 Clarendon Road, 1925-1929 23
    Interlude II: Gerald Finzi (1901-1956) 29
Chapter Three: 8 East Heath Road
        and 34 Willoughby Road, 1929-1938 33
    Interlude III: Ashmansworth (1938) 42
Chapter Four: 106 Wildwood Road,
        pre-war and war years, 1939-1945 46
    Interlude IV: The National Gallery Concerts 57
Chapter Five: 106 Wildwood Road,
        post-war years, 1945-1972 63
    Interlude V: Arnold van Wyk (1916–1983) 82
Chapter Six: Corpus Christi College, 1972 85
Chapter Seven: 51 Barton Road, Cambridge 1973- . . 90

Postlude: Music Autographs and Sources 97
Recordings 106
Index 108

Illustrations between pages 66-67

To my Friends

Preface

What follows has relied mainly on a very fallible memory. Memory, however, has been stimulated by pocket engagement-books (*not* diaries) that I have kept from 1925 until today. (For some unknown reason the one for 1961 is missing.)

Some of the material has already appeared in earlier publications, namely: *The Music of Howard Ferguson*, ed. Alan Ridout (Thames Publishing, 1989); *Recorded Sound* (The Institute of Recorded Sound, Spring 1962); *Music and Letters* (April 1957); *O Rare Hoffnung* (Putnam & Co Ltd, 1960); *Myra Hess by her Friends* (Hamish Hamilton, 1966); and *Acta Academica*, ed. IJ Grové (The University of the Orange Free State, Bloemfontein, 1984). My thanks are due to the respective editors and publishers for giving permission for the material to be reprinted here.

My warmest thanks are due to Catherine Walters for her expert typing, and to John Bishop of Thames Publishing, who has been so helpful throughout.

HOWARD FERGUSON
Cambridge, 1997

Chapter One: Beginnings
1908-1925

Though I cannot vouch for it myself, I'm told that one of my earliest pleasures was being lifted up to our ancient Collard & Collard upright piano (a wedding-present to my parents), and allowed to bang the keys with my fists. Perhaps more significantly, at the age of six I clamoured to have piano lessons with the young lady who was trying to teach my two unwilling sisters.

The family was not musical – though I can just remember my mother playing piano pieces she had learnt at a finishing-school in Brussels and my father fingering his way through 'There is a tavern in the town' from *The Student's Song Book*. Yet my remarkable parents never failed to give every help and encouragement to the strange child whose arrival in their midst had not, I gather, been entirely intentional. I was born in Belfast, Northern Ireland, on 21 October 1908, the fifth and last child of Stanley Ferguson, a banker, and his much-loved wife Frances. Her father had for many years been Managing Director of the Ulster Bank; and my father, having started as the bank's solicitor, eventually followed in his footsteps. The interests of the family tended towards golf and other sporting activities; in spite of this, my two brothers and two sisters were remarkably tolerant of a sibling whose concerns were so different from theirs.

Belfast was not an unmusical city, even in those pre-BBC days. The Belfast Philharmonic Society, part-professional and part-amateur, gave four or five choral and orchestral concerts each season, including the inevitable *Messiah* at Christmas. In addition, there were occasional chamber-music recitals by local players or visitors from England, and a series of celebrity concerts presenting international luminaries such as Pachmann and Tetrazzini. (Having been thrilled by a scratchy gramophone record of Tetrazzini singing 'Je suis Titania' from Ambroise Thomas' *Mignon*, I was grievously disappointed it was not included in her programme, even as an encore.) Greatly looked forward to were the annual visits of the Carl Rosa and Joseph O'Mara opera companies, who staged not only the local favourites, *The Bohemian*

Girl and *Maritana*, but also surprisingly out-of-the-way works. The very first opera my parents took me to was Nicolai's *Merry Wives of Windsor* – which I didn't manage to hear again for another fifty years – and before reaching my teens I had already seen Wagner's *Tannhäuser* and *Lohengrin*.

Being the odd-man-out in a family is a dubious distinction; but as far as I was concerned it had the inestimable advantage of making me the sole charge of my beloved nanny, May Cunningham, known as Pu (short for Pussycat). She came from farming stock in County Monaghan, was small and bright, had slight curvature of the spine (which I never noticed until I was in my twenties), and possessed the sweetest nature imaginable. She arrived on the scene just in time to save the life of my sickly month-old self, and from that moment a special link seems to have been forged between us.

On reaching the age of six I went off in my sisters' care to the kindergarten department of the school they attended. There I had the good fortune to be spotted by one of the two best piano teachers in Belfast, by name Frederick J Sawyer. A small, peppery man, but a good musician, he was organist of Elmwood Presbyterian Church, which my family attended irregularly. Besides his private pupils he took the singing classes at the school. During these he occasionally threw in some questions regarding the music that was being sung; and as they tended to be answered by a small boy, seated cross-legged in the front row, Mr Sawyer became interested. He got in touch with my parents, suggested that I should come to him for piano lessons, and as a result I enjoyed four years of solid grounding in piano technique and the rudiments of music. The lessons even continued when I became a boarder at Rockport, a preparatory school beautifully situated on the shores of Belfast Lough, for I was allowed to escape once a week and make the journey to and from Belfast by train.

The piano wasn't the only instrument I was interested in. I cajoled my long-suffering parents into buying a small harmonium, on condition that I repaid its vast cost (£30) out of future birthday and Christmas presents. It was duly installed in the nursery, where I could play it to my heart's content without disturbing the rest of the family.

The violin also exercised a powerful fascination. So much so that, although no carpenter, I determined to make one for myself. It consisted of a flat piece of wood some fifteen inches in length. Pegholes were bored with the aid of a red-hot poker; strings – real violin strings bought from a music shop – were stretched over a home-made bridge; and a bow was contrived from a curved branch of a garden shrub plus a hank of hair extracted from the tail of the family rocking-horse. It was an enterprising effort: but for some reason it never *sounded* quite right.

Much more satisfactory was the three-quarter-size violin on which, at the age of eight, I began lessons with Miss Winifred Burnett, leader of the Belfast Philharmonic Orchestra, who had studied in Leipzig and was herself a fine teacher.

In due course I was entered for the appropriate piano and violin classes in the Belfast Musical Competitions. This annual event was run by music enthusiasts, both professional and amateur, of whom I have good reason to remember two: Mrs Bessie Moore, a retired opera singer married to a Belfast doctor; and Mrs Jack MacIlwaine, who will enter the story at a later stage.

The adjudicator of the piano classes in 1922 was Harold Samuel, whose remarkable Bach Week in London I had recently read about in the *Musical Times* (see p 16) It was therefore a special thrill to see the great man in the flesh, seated on a dais above the audience, looking dapper, if slightly forbidding, in a well-cut grey suit. Even more exciting was the fact that he gave me a prize for playing the first movement of the Mozart A minor Piano Sonata and Frank Bridge's *Rosemary*, and afterwards intimated that he would like to meet my parents. This was easily arranged, for he was staying with Mrs Moore, who had been a fellow-student at the Royal College of Music; and she in turn knew me from the days when I took part in the children's operettas that she produced. My mother and I were invited round for coffee one evening, Mr Samuel played for us and proved to be not in the least forbidding, and a further meeting was arranged to include my father. On this occasion Mr Samuel suggested that I ought to take music seriously (I had never thought of doing anything else), and added that I should go to London without delay to work at piano with him prior to entering the Royal College of Music. I can never get over the fact that my mother and father immediately agreed to this startling proposition.

Thus at the age of 13½ I left my preparatory school, and in great excitement was taken to London by my parents, who happened to be going there already on one of my father's business trips.

Soon after our arrival we met the delightful Californian family with whom it had been arranged I should stay. They lived at 7 Lansdowne Road, Holland Park, a comfortable, stuccoed Victorian corner-house with a short garden at the back. The head of the family was Mrs Denis O'Sullivan (Bess), widow of an Irish-American baritone who had earlier made a great success in the London run of Stanford's opera *Shamus O'Brien*. A brisk, intelligent woman, with hair worn in a curious little topknot secured by a small black ribbon, her friends tended to be involved one way or another in the arts. She herself had written a novel which doubtless I read, but of which I remember no more than its title, *Mr Dymock*. More to my taste was her typewritten Life of her husband, with its absorbing account of the great San Francisco earthquake and fire of 1904. Her daughter Biddy, just turned twenty, was a dear person. She could have been a brilliant cartoonist, but preferred animals and kept a dozen hens and an alarmingly large Alsatian dog in the garden. The son Terence, nearing the end of his last term at Westminster School, was exclusively interested in rowing. (There was an elder son, Curtis, whom I never met, as he was a business-man in America.)

The highlight of that first magical week in London – apart from a never-to-be-forgotten fresh *pêche melba* at a lunch with Mr Samuel – was a visit to Covent Garden, where the newly formed British National Opera Company was holding its first season. *Parsifal* was included in the repertoire; and although I already knew it well from playing the vocal score and singing all the roles, male and female, I had of course never seen it. It must have been the last thing in the world my parents would have chosen to go to; but in their usual self-denying way, they took me to it and gave me my greatest operatic experience to date.

After my mother and father had returned to Ireland I settled down happily with the O'Sullivans. They had no piano; but Mr Samuel came to the rescue by lending me a little Bechstein upright he had been given some years before. In the mornings I went to a crammer in preparation for the entrance examination to Westminster School, where it had been decided I should go; in the afternoons I practised and did homework.

It was all so totally unlike anything I had experienced before that it was hard to believe what was happening. There were the exciting lessons with Mr Samuel; the fascinatingly unfamiliar food provided by Mrs O'Sullivan, who was a good cook; and of course London itself. Indeed, the only thing that clouded my happiness was news of the departure of my beloved Pu from the family home in Belfast, where she had worked for thirteen years but was no longer needed.

Arrival in England also enabled me to follow a hobby that was begun by the chance purchase of a sixpenny booklet on wireless telegraphy while I was still at prep school. It was in the days before the BBC; but with the help of an outside aerial, erected precariously on the roof of No 7 by Biddy and myself, a pair of earphones, and a primitive crystal set made out of the cardboard container of a Dictaphone cylinder and what appeared to be miles of wire, I was able to hear the test-transmissions from 2LO, the Marconi Company's station at Chelmsford in Essex. The connection with music may seem remote; yet one of the first things I happened on was an early performance of Mahler's *Das Lied von der Erde* given by Adrian Boult in Birmingham, with Astra Desmond and Walter Widdop as soloists.

At about this time I was beginning to get interested in composition. Though not in the least precocious, I had always been fascinated by the *look* of the notes I wrote down, however meaningless they might be. Then, rather to my own surprise, during my first summer holiday in Ireland I produced a short piano piece with three or four variations.

On returning to London in September 1922 I set out for my first term as a day-boy at Westminster School, rigged out in the regulation Eton jacket, top hat, and carefully rolled umbrella. The Headmaster at that time was the Reverend Dr Harold Costley-White, later Dean of Gloucester. I'm told that he was not altogether popular with some of his staff, but he couldn't have been more helpful as far as I was concerned. This may have been due in part to his love of music; but more significant, I suspect, was the fact that Mr Samuel and Adrian Boult (who had himself been at the School) had earlier visited him to ask if I could be allowed some time off for piano practice. In answer, Dr Costley-White made the unheard-of concession of giving me leave to go home every day at lunchtime, thus missing all afternoon classes. This was specially remarkable since I was not going to be involved in any way with music-making in the school.

Two memorable domestic musical events took place during my stay with the O'Sullivans. The first was the result of Mr Samuel's offer to play, for the benefit of myself and anyone else who cared to listen, a slimmed-down version of the four operas of Wagner's *Ring*, spread over five or six weekly instalments. In spite of having turned the pages for him every evening I cannot for the life of me remember what was included and what left out; but the extracts were quite lengthy, and each one was prefaced by an account of the stage action involved. All this was done without any previous preparation on Mr Samuel's part, for his encyclopaedic knowledge of opera – as of every other kind of music – enabled him to devise the whole presentation as he went along.

In contrast, the second domestic event required a great deal of preparation. In 1913 Debussy wrote a children's ballet, *La boîte à joujoux*, for the amusement of his small daughter Chou-Chou; it was published as a piano score with delightful illustrations by André Hellé, and concerned the love-life of a doll and a wooden soldier. As soon as I played it to Biddy O'Sullivan she determined to put on a performance in their large double drawing-room, with me as pianist. She gathered together a number of young friends of the family, allotted the parts – The Doll was played by a flaxen-haired Monica Dickens, later famous as a novelist, and The Little Soldier by her sister Dodie – rehearsals were arranged, and costumes made; a curtain was even rigged up to divide the two halves of the drawing-room. When the performance at last took place, everyone enjoyed themselves hugely, and the audience (mostly consisting of the children's parents) was gratifyingly appreciative.

The following summer saw Terence O'Sullivan's final term at Westminster, and the family's departure for a lengthy holiday with relatives in California. It also left me without a London base. Once again Mr Samuel came to the rescue by offering me a place in the home he was about to set up at 12 Inglis Road, Ealing, for his mother, an unmarried sister, and a nephew and niece. I was extremely grateful, not least because I sensed it might provide an opportunity to be reunited with my dear Pu. Mrs Samuel was in her eighties, frail and in need of constant care. What more natural than my suggestion that Pu should come and look after her? – a plan that was soon arranged.

Attendance at Westminster continued for another three terms, at the end of which (at the nowadays unbelievably early age of 15½) I was mercifully allowed to leave. I don't think I learnt a great deal during the years I was there – apart from the skill of rolling an umbrella – but I did whatever work was necessary, kept out of trouble, and looked forward impatiently to the day when I would be free to go to the Royal College of Music. Not being gregarious I made few friends at school. Indeed, the only one I remember is Anthony Gishford, who by a strange chance was to become a Director of Boosey & Hawkes, the firm that was eventually my publisher.

Entering the RCM in the summer term of 1924 gave existence a new sense of both freedom and purpose. My classes, so far as I can remember, were fitted into three days in the week, which left plenty of time for work at home, where the little Bechstein was installed in my bedroom, and a model 'A' size grand, loaned to Mr Samuel by Steinways, occupied the living room.

The Director of the College, Sir Hugh Allen, was also Professor of Music at Oxford, a Fellow of New College, and a power in the land. (It was rumoured that he made all important organ appointments in England.) His brusque manner, bristling moustache and beetling brows could be intimidating; but there was another, less public, side to him. In order to show young Douglas Fox that the loss of an arm during the 1914 war need not be the end of his career as an organist, Allen invited Fox to New College Chapel, where he (Allen) played the whole of a service with one arm tied behind his back.

Among notable Professors at the RCM were the composers Vaughan Williams, John Ireland, Herbert Howells, George Dyson and R O Morris (always known as 'R O', because he so disliked his names, Reginald Owen); and the pianists Marmaduke Barton, Herbert Fryer and Harold Samuel (the latter was so often away on concert tours that his pupils were apt to receive most of their lessons from someone else). The First Orchestra was conducted by Adrian Boult, and the Second by Malcolm Sargent. The most outstanding student at that time, both as conductor and composer, was Constant Lambert, soon to be commissioned by Diaghilev to write his *Romeo and Juliet* for the Russian Ballet. His exact contemporary Michael Tippett was also there, but as an unusually late developer he had not yet made much mark. The influences most strongly felt by students were probably Vaughan Williams, Holst, French composers, Sibelius, and perhaps Bartok; for

Schönberg, Webern and Berg were only beginning to emerge in England as significant figures.

My own principal teachers were R O Morris for harmony, counterpoint and composition; and Malcolm Sargent for conducting. Meanwhile, piano was continued privately with Mr Samuel.

Morris, who was better known as a teacher than a composer, had recently published his remarkable book, *Contrapuntal Technique in the 16th Century* (Clarendon Press, Oxford 1922). It had an immense influence on teaching in England and elsewhere, for he was the first to point out that the study of counterpoint should be based on the works of those who wrote it, rather than on arbitrary rules invented by theorists such as Fux and Rockstro. It was, however, too advanced for a beginner like myself; and since R O disliked the textbooks of Kitson, Macpherson, *et al*, he used laboriously to write out on my manuscript paper the rules that were to be learnt. Their conciseness and clarity were so typical of him that, by way of a 'portrait', I printed them many years later in an article entitled 'Early Lessons with R O' in the *RCM Magazine* of Summer 1987.

I found him an immensely stimulating composition teacher. He instantly spotted the weak link in any chain of musical thought, but never imposed, or even suggested, an actual solution. Thus a pupil was allowed to develop along his own lines, without being burdened (as with so many teachers) by a single overpowering influence. His approach was slightly impersonal: cool rather than over-enthusiastic, yet never discouraging. I could scarcely believe my ears when one day, much later, he said in his slow, quiet voice, 'Yes, Howard, I like that.'

Sargent was the exact opposite. A total extrovert, he had recently made his name by being invited by Sir Henry Wood to conduct a work of his own, *Impressions on a Windy Day*, at a Prom concert. I don't know whether the piece was of any musical value, but the performance showed that he was a born conductor. Choirs and amateur orchestras adored him, for he could make them sing and play better than they knew how. Professionals, on the other hand, sensed a basic superficiality and unkindly dubbed him 'Flash Harry'. Nevertheless, he was an exciting teacher of conducting, for he had codified the practical techniques involved, and this enabled him to pass them on to his students. He held two related classes every week. At one, a pair of students played respectively the string and wind parts of a work on two pianos, reading from full scores, while a third did his best to conduct their efforts. At the other, each aspirant rehearsed a movement with the Third Orchestra (consisting entirely of second-study players), while Sargent stood on the rostrum beside him (or her), making comments. It could be an unnerving experience: particularly as one was never quite sure whether the sounds that emerged were to be blamed on the conductor or the orchestra.

Though chamber-music classes were not generally available to anyone who studied their instrument outside the College, they could be taken as an 'extra'. This I did, as Mr Samuel was anxious I should have the benefit of working with his old friend Ivor James. Mr James, universally known as Jimmy, was the principal cello Professor at College and a chamber-music player of vast experience. The piano trio of which I formed a part learnt an enormous amount from him. He seemed to know the entire repertoire from memory, as was startlingly evident when he would stand at the far end of the classroom, with no score in hand, and say, 'Now begin that passage again, three bars before figure 17'.

One of the great attractions of the College was being able to walk into any orchestral or opera rehearsal and hear an unfamiliar work as often as one wished. My most memorable experience in that direction was to go to many of the preliminary rehearsals of Vaughan Williams' new opera *Hugh the Drover*, and thus get to know it inside out. I also of course heard the first performance in July 1924 – which proved to be the earliest of some fifteen first performances of his works that I was to hear over the years.

Interlude I: Harold Samuel (1879-1937)

Harold Samuel only narrowly escaped being turned into an infant prodigy. His complaisant father enjoyed taking his six-year-old son to smoking-concerts and parading his precocious talents before admiring friends. On one such occasion the boy was asked to play an accompaniment for a singer he had never met before. The man was so enormous it was unthinkable he could be anything but a basso profundo. Unfortunately, when Handel's *O ruddier than the cherry* began in a piping male-alto voice, young Harold was so overcome with laughter that he had to be removed from the platform. Thereafter his mother, being a sensible woman, decreed that his studies should be uninterrupted by smoking-concerts.

Samuel was 17 years old when he entered the Royal College of Music to study piano with Edward Dannreuther and composition with Charles Villiers Stanford. In view of his eventual career it is surprising that at first he should have been known mainly as a player of Liszt. Soon he became interested in a wider range of music, and virtually abandoned the purely virtuoso repertoire. Altogether characteristic is the fact that he became one of the coaches in the opera class, and was involved in the earliest English performance of Verdi's *Falstaff*, given by students of the RCM under Stanford at His Majesty's Theatre.

Shortly after leaving the College, Samuel gave his first recital, on 14 March 1900 at the former Steinway Hall in Wigmore Street, where he startled his audience by devoting the main part of the programme to Bach's hour-long *'Goldberg' Variations*. Today this would cause little surprise; but at that time Bach was comparatively unfamiliar to concert-goers. His keyboard music was rarely heard other than in arrangements by Liszt, Tausig or Busoni; and even as familiar a work as the *St Matthew Passion* was never performed complete in London until 1926, when it was given by Sir Henry Wood at the Queen's Hall with students of the Royal Academy of Music.

In spite of the success of this first recital, Samuel was forced for the moment to abandon the hazardous career of a soloist, for the early death of his father had left him with unexpected financial responsibilities. Instead, he turned to the securer if less glamorous work of accompanying and teaching. His outstanding musicianship soon made him one of the most sought-after accompanists in London; but opportunities for solo work remained few and far between, for concert-organisers and the public have always been unwilling to admit that someone can excel as both accompanist and soloist. Realising this hard truth, Samuel took a remarkably courageous step on reaching the age of 40: he entirely gave up accompanying and determined to devote himself exclusively to solo work.

By way of announcing the fact, he gave his second solo recital. This was at the Wigmore Hall in 1919 and consisted entirely of Bach. In the event he had no reason to regret his quixotic decision, for the recital was an enormous musical and personal success, and marked the beginning of his world-wide career.

Two years later, in 1921, he embarked on an even more unusual project, which many people assured him was totally impractical. He gave six Bach recitals on six consecutive days, playing entirely from memory. The programmes were as follows:

Wigmore Hall: Week of Bach Recitals

Monday, 30 May 1921

Partita in A minor
Five Preludes & Fugues from the '48'
Fantasia and Fugue in A minor
French Suite in E

Tuesday, 31 May 1921

Toccata in D
Overture in the French Style
Two Preludes & Fugues from the '48'
Fantasia in C minor
French Suite in E flat

Wednesday, 1 June 1921

English Suite in G minor
Toccata in C minor
Partita in B flat
Two Preludes & Fugues from the '48'

Thursday, 2 June 1921

Toccata in F sharp minor
Short Prelude in C
Two Bourrées from English Suite in A
Short Preludes in C minor and D
Toccata in G minor
Three Preludes & Fugues
   from the '48'
Partita in G

Friday, 3 June 1921   *Saturday, 4 June 1921*

Prelude, Fugue & Allegro in E flat	Chromatic Fantasia & Fugue
Aria with 30 Variations ('The Goldberg')	Partita in C minor
	Three Preludes & Fugues from the '48'
Invention in B flat	
Chorale Prelude 'Wachet auf!'	French Suite in G

Before the week was out, the recitals had reached the headlines of the evening papers. More importantly, they opened the eyes of the public, and of musicians themselves, to the vast treasure-house of Bach's keyboard music.

Following this sensational success, Samuel was invited by Sir Hugh Allen, Director of the RCM, to collaborate with Donald Francis Tovey in a new edition of Bach's *48 Preludes and Fugues*, to be published by The Associated Board of the Royal Schools of Music. (Legend has it that Samuel knew them all from memory, but this is not true.) He was apprehensive about the idea from the outset: for while he had the greatest admiration for Tovey as a scholar, he did not always see eye-to-eye with him regarding performance. A seemingly endless correspondence ensued between London and Edinburgh, where Tovey was Reid Professor of Music at the University; yet the longer it went on the more points of disagreement emerged. Finally Samuel decided that, since he was busy with concert work at the time, the best thing to do would be to take a night train to Edinburgh, spend a whole day discussing the various problems with Tovey, and return the next night. When he got there Tovey welcomed him warmly, talked throughout the day most interestingly on every topic under the sun except Bach's '48', and, half an hour before the train back to London was due to leave, said with a bland smile, 'But my dear Harold, I must not *digress*'. At which point Harold realised that the collaboration was a chimera. On his return to London he phoned Allen and resigned from the project. Sir Hugh was horrified, said they couldn't possibly do the edition without him, and implored him to change his mind. Finally he asked: 'Would you at least do the fingering?' Harold pointed out that, because of his huge hands, his fingering was very unusual and would be useless to anyone else. 'Never mind', said Allen, 'that's what we want.' Which explains why the fingering in the early Associated Board edition of the '48' is sometimes rather unexpected.

In all, Samuel gave six Bach Weeks in London, always varying the programmes, and one in New York with equal success. In later years he restricted himself to single recitals, partly because the mental and physical strain of a whole week was excessive, and partly because he felt his missionary work had already achieved its aim.

If asked why he played Bach on the piano rather than the harpsichord, he gave two reasons. First, he felt that the piano was the true descendant of Bach's favourite keyboard instrument, the clavichord: for the strings of both clavichord and piano are *struck*, and can therefore produce continuously graded dynamics; whereas those of the harpsichord are *plucked*, and can only produce dynamics in discrete steps by means of a change of stop or manual. His second reason is best told in his own words. After one of his New York recitals the great harpsichordist Wanda Landowska came to the artistes' room. She expatiated at length on the beauty of his performance, and even more on the desirability of playing Bach on the harpsichord. Harold listened patiently to the torrent of words until finally, in a momentary lull, he heard himself say with more honesty than tact, 'But Madame Landowska, I don't *like* the harpsichord!'

It's interesting to find in the 1990s that fashions in performance have begun to come full circle; for even the severest scholars and critics are now able to admit that the piano, if treated sensitively and musically (as does András Schiff, for example), is a perfectly valid medium for the music of Bach and his contemporaries.

Samuel never had any wish to be known as a 'Bach specialist'. Indeed, he intensely disliked the label, which must have been particularly galling to a musician of his wide range and sympathies. He was always ready to play almost anything from the Elizabethan virginalists to Ravel, with Brahms and Debussy as special favourites. Further than Ravel he was less inclined to go, as was shown by an embarrassing occasion in 1924. His old friend Frank Bridge had recently completed a piano sonata and was anxious for Harold to give the first performance. But when Frank played the work to him, Harold found himself so out of sympathy with it that he thought it wiser not to do so. (In fact, the première was given by Myra Hess.)

He had a phenomenal memory and could sit down and play virtually anything you mentioned, whether it was piano music, orchestral music, song or opera. He was, too, a superb chamber-music player, who always delighted string players by providing the support they needed without ever swamping them.

Like most performers, he suffered acutely from nerves, though no one would have suspected it from the buoyant way he walked on to a platform. They took the form, so surprising in the possessor of an exceptional memory, of being terrified of having a memory-lapse. Of course he never did. But since 'forgetting' for him meant leaving out a single note from a chord, perhaps the fear is understandable.

During the twenty years before he became a soloist, Samuel wrote a certain amount of music, including songs and a musical comedy that had a London run. By far his greatest success, however, was acknowledged on the printed copy merely as 'Arranged by HS.' It arose in a curious way. One of his fellow-members of the Savage Club in London was Frederick E Weatherley, a lawyer also well known as a writer of sentimental song-lyrics. One day Weatherley said to him, 'Harold, I've just written words and a piano accompaniment for a rather nice tune I've come across: would you be a good chap and see if the piano part's all right?' Harold looked, saw it was far from all right, and offered to provide a new one there and then. After half an hour at a desk in the smoking-room of the club the new accompaniment was finished, and in due course the song was published. A year or so later they met again. Weatherley said, 'That song with your accompaniment seems to be going rather well. How about having a proper contract and dividing the royalties 50/50?' Harold thanked him, and for the rest of his life received an annual royalty that grew larger and larger as the years passed. The song's enormous success is less surprising when one learns that Weatherley's 'rather nice tune' was *The Londonderry Air*, and the words he wrote for it the immensely popular *Danny Boy*. After telling me this story, Harold added the advice, '*Always* keep your share of the copyright in anything you've written!'

As a teacher Samuel was more concerned with music than with technique as such. When I first came to him he made sure that I had 'done my scales and arpeggios' with Mr Sawyer in Belfast, then said there was no need for me to practise them endlessly. Nor was he keen on mechanically repeated 'exercises' of the Czerny type. Far better to devise one's own exercises out of the music one was working at, for those would be relevant to the problems involved. The essential thing was to recognise the requirements of the music itself. Once these were clear in one's mind, the difficulties had a way of solving themselves. If not, it was then time to start analysing precisely what hand-movements were needed to achieve a particular result.

The earliest of Samuel's overseas tours took him to South Africa in the summer and autumn of 1922. For the first couple of months he examined for The Associated Board of the Royal Schools of Music; he then gave a series of recitals, one of which was enlivened by two burly kaffirs carrying a sofa through the concert-hall during one of the quieter items.

Early in 1924 he made his first trip to America, in answer to an invitation from Mrs Elizabeth Sprague Coolidge to take part in a chamber-music festival she was sponsoring in April at the Ojai Valley in California. Before that came his first New York recital, on the very morning of which he received a cable from England to say that his mother had died. It was a terrible blow, for they had been devoted to one another. Nevertheless he determined not to cancel the recital, which he duly gave in the Town Hall (a concert hall).

It so happened that in the audience was a music-loving lawyer, Hartwell Cabell, with his wife Louise. They had never met Samuel; but on hearing of his loss they went round to the artiste's room after the concert, introduced themselves, and with typical American warmth invited him to stay with them for the rest of his visit. He did so, and thus began a friendship that lasted for the rest of his life.

Most people who met Harold would have thought of him as a consistently jovial and ebullient character, always ready to entertain friends with a ridiculous anecdote or limerick (often rather blue), or even break out into a Victorian music-hall ditty:

> Yer baby has gone down the plughole,
> Yer baby has gone down the plug;
> > The pore little thing
> > Was so skinny and thin
> It should 'ave been bathed in a j-hug.

Yet there was another side to the coin. Hard though it is to believe, during the four years we were to live in Clarendon Road, Harold every night insisted on Pu hiding all the knives in the house, as he was terrified of walking in his sleep and killing somebody.

More understandable, because of the family's early dependence on him, was his lifelong fear of financial insecurity. Not that he was in the least mean – quite the reverse; but ever since I got to know him he took on far too much work, 'in case he hadn't enough engagements to make ends meet'. Indeed, that was probably what in the end led to his comparatively early death.

Chapter Two: 12 Clarendon Road
1925-1929

When Harold returned from his first trip to America in the late autumn of 1924 it was to completely changed domestic circumstances. He had never felt particularly close to his family, apart from his beloved mother; and now that she had died he was anxious to set up an establishment of his own, with my former nanny, Pu, as housekeeper and me as fortunate lodger. The ideal dwelling was found at 12 Clarendon Road, Holland Park, not far from 7 Lansdowne Road, where I had lived with the O'Sullivans. The late-Victorian house was semi-detached, the two upper floors being occupied by the landlord's elderly brother and sister, and the two lower rented by Harold. The special attraction was a large single-storied studio built out into the garden at the back, which immediately became a spacious music-room containing two Steinway grand pianos. The Bechstein upright lived in the dining-room on the floor above, at a sufficient distance from the studio to allow both of us to work at the same time without disturbing one another.

Housekeeper Pu's helpers at first consisted of a rather prim parlour-maid (they were still obtainable in those days) and a cook, both of whom came in daily. After some time the cook departed, and Pu's niece, Betty Cunningham, came from Ireland to tide us over temporarily. This was such a success that she stayed until she died thirty years later. She and Pu managed the cooking between them, being taught by Harold. He was a brilliantly inventive cook – though it was essential for someone to write down the recipes he created, for subsequent 'improvements' were not always so successful.

Harold greatly enjoyed entertaining friends; and after an excellent dinner the party would repair to the studio, where they would be mercilessly subjected to two-piano music. On one stifling summer evening, with all the doors and windows open, we embarked on Ravel's *La Valse* well after midnight. Next morning a plaintive note came from our next-door neighbour, saying she would be *so* grateful if we didn't play *quite* so late at night, as her two daughters did brain-work during the day. Harold hastened round with profuse apologies, only to be met with the assurance that they *loved* listening to our music.

In June 1925, towards the end of my first year at the RCM, I entered for an open composition scholarship. The examination was in two parts, the first of which took place in a murky upstairs room in the nearby Albert Hall. There the candidates were invited to write some variations on a given theme. (As I was unaccustomed to working away from the piano, my contribution must have been pretty odd.) For the second part of the examination we were interviewed one by one at the RCM and asked to improvise on the piano – which is something I've never been able to do. Seeing that I was at a loss, Sir Hugh Allen, chairman of the examiners, encouraged me to illustrate the episode in Shaw's *St Joan* when the wind changes direction on the banks of the Loire. After I had rippled on for some minutes in a vaguely aquatic manner, Sir Hugh mercifully brought the session to an end by saying, 'Thank you very much: that will do.' In spite of these disasters I did win the scholarship: so presumably the examiners must have found the compositions I had submitted less discouraging.

A year later came my first two professional engagements as a pianist. Harold had been booked to give a joint recital at Oundle School with the singer Carrie Tubb, a well-known dramatic soprano for whom he had often played in the past; and she very sweetly agreed to his suggestion that I should be her accompanist. Oundle was one of the first public schools to make a special feature of music, and recently the enterprising Director of Music, Clement Spurling, had created a stir by giving a performance of the Bach B minor Mass in which the entire school took part. Carrie Tubb's son was a boarder at the school, so naturally she was invited to be the soprano soloist. By the time of our concert she was nearing the end of her public career; but she was still a magnificent singer, and it was a great experience for a teenager like myself to be allowed to play for her. Moreover, she was an exceedingly nice person, who made my first appearance as an accompanist positively enjoyable.

The second engagement, even more exciting for me, was to give a programme of two-piano music with Harold himself at the country home of his American friends the Navarros. Antonio de Navarro was a cultivated New Yorker of Basque descent. In the mid-1890s he had married the American actress Mary Anderson, who, though only 28 when she retired from the stage, already had audiences throughout the United States and Great Britain at her feet. (My father saw her act when he was a student at Trinity College, Dublin, and confirmed my suspicion that it was her astonishing beauty rather than her dramatic gift that accounted for her fame.) On marrying they made their home at Court Farm in the village of Broadway in Worcestershire – then a quiet haunt for artists rather than the tourist bedlam of today – by building a magnificent music-room to join together two small 15th-century farmhouses, where a beautiful garden at the back rose up the lower slopes of Broadway Hill. Throughout the years countless artists, writers and musicians were made welcome, among them Henry James and Rossetti in the early days, and Bernard Shaw, Masefield and Elgar more recently. Our programme consisted of Mozart's two-piano Sonata and the Brahms *Haydn Variations*, with a group of solos from Harold in the middle.

Such musical events were generally held to celebrate the birthday of the Navarros' son Toty (José Maria); though not on this occasion, for he was away from home. However, I met him some months later when we returned to Court Farm on a visit. He was then 30 years old, a Fellow of Trinity College, Cambridge, and already a well-known archaeologist. Though not conventionally good-looking, he possessed enormous charm and an enthusiasm that was irresistible. He claimed he never felt at ease with teenagers, yet he and I got on together particularly well from the moment we met, and he was to remain one of my closest friends until his death some 50 years later. Poetry and music were his two great passions, with Brahms the hero of his personal pantheon. In relaxed moments he was a brilliant raconteur and a deadly mimic. When first I met one of his victims – a young Cambridge lady long since dead – I had the greatest difficulty in keeping a straight face, so exact had been his imitation of her peculiar voice and manner of speech.

Early in 1927 Harold had been booked for a four-month tour in the USA, to include a Bach Week in New York. As he was going to be away for so long, he decided to rent an apartment there and take along Pu to look after it. And as my composition teacher R O Morris had recently become head of the Theory Department at the Curtis Institute in Philadelphia, Harold suggested to my parents that I should go too, so that lessons with Morris and himself should not be interrupted. They most helpfully agreed. We crossed from Liverpool to New York on the Cunarder *Celtic*, and installed ourselves in a pleasant apartment at 410 West End Avenue, found for us by Louise Cabell.

I used to go to Philadelphia once a fortnight, have a lesson with R O in the morning, lunch with him and his wife, and return to New York in the afternoon. On one memorable occasion I stayed overnight to hear Rachmaninov give the first performance of his Fourth Piano Concerto with Stokowski and the Philadelphia Orchestra. The work itself was not particularly exciting, but I thought, and still think, that Rachmaninov was the most remarkable pianist I have ever heard.

This was only one of many memorable musical occasions, for I found myself being taken to either a concert or an opera by various kind friends of Harold's on almost every alternate night of our stay. Being accustomed to the lax orchestral playing then endemic in England, it was a revelation to hear the magnificently trained orchestras of New York, Philadelphia, Boston and Chicago, under conductors such as Toscanini, Koussevitsky, Frederick Stock and Bruno Walter. The high point came when I was smuggled into Carnegie Hall one morning for a Toscanini rehearsal of Beethoven's Ninth Symphony. It was doubly memorable as being the first time I saw Toscanini conduct, and the first time I heard sense made of the symphony's choral finale, with its terrifying demands on the singers.

Among operas seen were *Boris Godunov* with Chaliapine, *Rosenkavalier* with Lotte Lehmann, Elizabeth Schumann, Maria Olczewska and Richard Meyer, both at the old Metropolitan Opera House on 40th Street; and more surprising, if less rewarding, Honegger's *Judith* in Boston with the 53-year-old Mary Garden, Debussy's favourite Mélisande, in the title role.

Picture galleries were another great attraction. I had recently become fascinated by early Italian and Flemish painting, through having fallen in love with the Fra Angelico predella of *Angels, Saints and Martyrs* in the London National Gallery. Our New York apartment was just across Central Park from the Metropolitan Museum; so after working in the morning I often took the little single-decker crosstown bus to spend the afternoon there or at the nearby Frick Collection. (The Museum of Modern Art and the Guggenheim Gallery had not yet been built.) Other great collections were visited when Harold happened to be playing in Boston, Chicago or Washington. And one evening, when we were being entertained by a wealthy couple, I found to my astonishment that I was sitting beside a miraculous little *Portrait of a Man* by Hans Memlinc.

The four-month visit was in every way a wonderful experience for an 18-year-old, and I enjoyed every minute of it; yet, strangely enough, it made me realise how very much I was attached to England.

On our return from New York, Harold rented a cottage for the summer months at Capel in Surrey, not far from Leith Hill. It was a delightful idea – the only drawback being that he himself, because of professional engagements, could rarely be there. However, it was near enough London for me to go up weekly for the beginning of my final year at the RCM; and as RO was still in Philadelphia, Vaughan Williams (his brother-in-law) most helpfully agreed to take me on for composition. It was a privilege to get to know him, for one felt that VW was still a great man, even if he had never written a note of music. Yet as far as I was concerned he was a less helpful teacher than RO. Not that he was unsympathetic or discouraging: but simply because RO's clarity of mind and slightly astringent approach were so stimulating. The first thing VW asked me to do was to write a double fugue in the style of a Handel chorus. I doubt if the fugue ever got finished; nevertheless, during the course of the year I learnt a great deal from him about unexpectedly practical matters, such as how to set out orchestral parts clearly, and other arcane topics.

By the time I left the RCM in 1928 my ambition to become a conductor had evaporated, for I lacked the quickness of mind and hearing to pinpoint mistakes during rehearsal. Nor did an insecure musical memory suggest a solo pianist's career. However, I had always loved playing chamber music; and that, plus some accompanying, was in future to provide a second string to compositional activities. It was an arrangement that worked surprisingly well: for, being an unprolific composer, I generally had a fallow year between one work and the next, and this could be occupied very agreeably, and not unprofitably, by performing chamber music.

During the same year the Oxford University Press issued the first of my works to appear in print: an arrangement for cello and piano of *Five Irish Folk Tunes*. They were written while I was still at College, and had been first performed by Ivor James at a Wigmore Hall recital on 25 October 1927, which also marked my first appearance as a pianist in a London concert hall. It was a nerve-wracking occasion for me; but I must confess my chief worry was over the absence of one of the two black buttons that should have decorated the back of my newly-tailored tail-coat suit.

Also written during College days was a setting for baritone and orchestra of 'A Lyke Wake Dirge', which, together with 'The Twa Corbies', later made up my *Two Ballads*, Op 1. The Dirge was first sung by Keith Falkner and conducted by Adrian Boult at a Sunday concert in Birmingham on 26 January 1930; but the *Ballads* were not heard as a pair until the 1934 Three Choirs Festival at Gloucester.

Interlude II: Gerald Finzi (1901-1956)

I first met Gerald Finzi in 1926. At that time he was studying 16th-century counterpoint (not composition) privately with R O Morris, my own composition teacher at the RCM. R O and his wife Jane had invited us both to tea, thinking (I suspect) that we might be good for one another. Gerald was seven years older than myself and had already published some songs. He was of medium height, had a swarthy complexion, a shock of short, dark, curly hair, and a vast amount of barely suppressed nervous energy. The occasion was enjoyable; but more significant was our second meeting. This took place quite by chance just outside the Albert Hall, where Richard Strauss had been conducting the BBC Orchestra in a concert of his own works, with the Mozart G minor Symphony thrown in for luck. The presence of the master himself should have guaranteed our seriousness; but I'm afraid the highlight of the evening had been during the noisiest climax of the *Alpine Symphony*, when the thunder-machine was seen to topple over and crash unheard into the middle of the startled orchestra. As the audience left the hall, Gerald and I cannoned into one another, both helpless with laughter; and from that moment our friendship was sealed.

For the next eight or nine years we generally met once a week at either his home or mine. We played through each other's compositions, discussed them, talked, and made music endlessly, for Gerald's curiosity about new or unfamiliar scores was insatiable. Being the less fluent pianist of the two, he would station himself at the extreme upper end of the keyboard and there play whatever vocal or instrumental part came his way, several octaves too high, rather loudly, and with a distinctly capricious sense of time-values. (He always vowed he had an excellent sense of rhythm, but that his fingers wouldn't do what his brain told them.) In this way we worked through enormous quantities of music of every style and period – operas, songs, chamber music and symphonies – the last in more orthodox but no less hectic duet arrangements. Occasionally, by way of relaxation, I was allowed to play a piece of genuine solo piano music.

It was Gerald who introduced me to the delights of the Queen's Hall, for hitherto I had been to surprisingly few orchestral concerts. We used to meet on the iron staircase that led to the box-office for the upper balcony, each pay our three shillings, and make for our favourite seats on the right- or left-hand side of the hall. (The seats were un-upholstered but not uncomfortable.) There we would avidly follow in our miniature scores whatever was being played, and thus gradually heard the standard orchestral repertoire and many first performances into the bargain – works such as Vaughan Williams' *Flos Campi*, *Sancta Civitas*, and Fourth Symphony: Ravel's Piano Concerto played by Marguerite Long (the conductor was the jockey-like Ravel himself); also Walton's First Symphony and Viola Concerto, the soloist in the latter being Paul Hindemith because Lionel Tertis, for whom the work had been written, said it was unplayable. Later, when it became extremely successful, he changed his tune and published a separate viola part 'bowed and fingered by Lionel Tertis'.

When I first knew Gerald he suffered from extreme uncertainty over matters of detail in his own works: not only in choosing between several slightly different versions of a phrase, but especially concerning dynamics and phrasing. With these latter he tended to solve the problem by leaving out such indications altogether, until it was pointed out to him that this didn't make the performer's life any easier. He would then agree, rather reluctantly, to the addition of a *piano* here and a *forte* there, with an occasional slur to show the beginning and end of a phrase, while muttering under his breath that the performer, if he were any sort of a musician, would instinctively do it like that anyway. It was only much later, with the experience gained from conducting his Newbury String Players (formed during the 1939 war), that he found it was essential to mark scores carefully, and learnt how to do so most efficiently.

In exchange for my suggested dynamics and phrase-marks, Gerald showed me how his very fast yet beautifully clear ink music-manuscript was written. He used a fairly broad nib and held the pen almost at right-angles to his forearm: a short sideways stroke would then automatically produce a thickish note-head, while an upward or downward stroke added a thin stem to the note without raising the pen from the paper.

Not long before Harold and I left for America, Gerald was told he had tuberculosis and would have to go into a sanatorium. This was a terrible shock, as nothing of the sort had been suspected before. On our return from New York he entered the King Edward VII Sanatorium at Midhurst in Sussex, at much the same time as we went to stay in Capel. Being in adjacent counties made it easy for me to cycle down and visit him in the sanatorium. To help pass the time he read a great deal; while I for my part sent him the Thomas Hardy posthumous poems, *Winter Words*, which were then being printed in the *Daily Telegraph*. (Some of them appear among his seventy Hardy settings.) He was also then much concerned with his *Fantasia for Piano and Strings*, later expanded into the *Grand Fantasia and Fugue for Piano and Orchestra*. His battling with the work under such circumstances so reminded me of David and Goliath that thereafter I always called him Dave. After three-and-a-half months in the sanatorium he was given a clean bill of health, and allowed to go home to resume his normal life.

Undoubtedly the most fortunate thing that ever happened to Gerald was his meeting with Joyce Black in 1933. He was having a working holiday at Lye Green in Sussex in a cottage rented from Joyce and her sister Mags, who lived nearby. Both sisters were tall and strikingly beautiful; but whereas Mags's chief concern was with horses, Joyce had worked at sculpture and pottery at the Central School of Art and Design, played the violin, and shared all Gerald's interests. It was no great surprise, therefore, when he told me that he and Joyce had become engaged.

After a honeymoon in Scotland they moved into 30 Downshire Hill, Hampstead, not far from 8 East Heath Road, where Harold and I then lived. This made weekly visits easy when Joy decided she would like to sculpt my head. The two of us would retire to their well-lit basement (where the modelling clay could be kept damp), and there she worked concentratedly for an hour or so, saying an occasional word to keep me awake. I was never allowed to look at the work-in-progress. But one evening, after a dozen sittings, I was led up to G's workroom at the top of the house, the door was flung open, and there I was in the dark, lying on a sofa with a powerful light trained on my white plaster face and a rug draped over some cushions to counterfeit my body.

With the idea of eventually building a house for themselves when they had found a suitable site, they temporarily took Beech Knoll in the village of Aldbourne in the middle of the Berkshire Downs. After several years of searching they found just what they wanted at Ashmansworth, high up on the Downs on the borders of Berkshire and Wiltshire, with a wonderful view to the south towards Winchester. There was already an ancient farmhouse there, but it was in such a dilapidated condition that it had to be pulled down. They could therefore make a fresh start with an architect friend, Peter Harland, who had already designed Arthur Bliss's country house, Penn Pits in Dorset. Under considerable pressure, Peter was persuaded to design the house Gerald and Joy wanted, rather than the house he would have preferred to build; but for some reason he absolutely refused to orientate it in exactly the direction they wished. To circumvent the problem, G & J drove up to the site one evening after the workmen had left, and quietly shifted all the pegs that showed where the walls should go. Later they told me gleefully that Peter had never noticed what they had done.

Chapter Three: 8 East Heath Road and 34 Willoughby Road 1929-1938

As Harold's lease of 12 Clarendon Road expired in 1929, we had to look around for a new home. Eventually the right place was found at 8 East Heath Road, a tall, detached, red-brick house facing two blocks of flats, The Pryors, which had been built (against all regulations) on the edge of the Heath itself. As the house was larger than we required, the top two floors were sub-let to Emmie Bass, a pillar of Harold's concert-agents, Messrs Ibbs & Tillett. My workroom, complete with Bechstein upright, was directly under the living-room of Miss Bass and her mother, so I often wondered what they must have thought of the sounds that percolated through the ceiling.

Once the lease for No 8 had been completed, Harold set off on another tour to South Africa. He left the move to me, and – perhaps more astonishingly – also the decorations of our new home. Yet on his return to England he expressed himself delighted with the latter though he *did* raise an eyebrow over the bathroom and downstairs cloakroom, both of which had been painted a rather startling *eau de Nil*.

I had already formed a piano trio with the cellist Helen Just (later to become the wife of her teacher, Ivor James) and the brilliant young violinist Eda Kersey, who tragically died of cancer in 1944. The trio was later expanded to form The Ensemble Players, whose aim (foreshadowing that of the present-day Nash Ensemble) was to perform chamber music for any number of players up to and including the Schubert Octet. The demand for large-scale combinations was limited; but one of our first engagements was to play piano quartets for the Oxford Music Club. The programme included the early William Walton and the Schumann, neither of which we had played before. Both were rehearsed without mishap; but unforeseen disaster awaited us in the Schumann. In the final bars of its slow movement the cello is required to lower the bottom string by a tone, in order to produce a beautifully rich B-flat octave. Alas, when it came to the performance,

Helen failed to lower the string quite low enough, with the result that an agonising B-flat/C-flat seventh emerged. Realising that nothing else could be done, she abandoned the low C-flat after a few seconds, to leave a somewhat less rich-sounding chord than Schumann had intended.

Pu and her niece Betty had come to look after us at East Heath Road; but shortly after our arrival, poor Betty became seriously ill with a complaint that mystified our nice new GP, Douglas Oakley. After some weeks of uncertainty he decided she should go into Bart's Hospital, where she was operated on successfully for a thyroid condition by a Mr Geoffrey Keynes. When I heard the name I thought, 'This can't possibly be the same man who edited the works of William Blake.' But indeed it was. Later, when I got to know him, and suggested that he must resent having to spend so much time cutting people up, he replied, 'Not at all! I *love* being awakened at 2 am in order to do an emergency appendix.'

He and his wife used to invite me to an early dinner at their house in Arkwright Road, after which we drove to Sadler's Wells to enjoy the ballet. Geoffrey was a keen balletomane, and had combined his two great enthusiasms by basing the scenario of Vaughan Williams's masque for dancing, *Job*, on Blake's engravings. After Sadler's Wells we would return to Arkwright Road, where he and I retired to his small study. Then, finding that I was a great admirer of Blake, he would go to a tallboy in the corner of the room, produce original after original, and place them in my hands. I could scarcely believe my eyes. His wonderful collection now belongs to the Fitzwilliam Museum in Cambridge, where a 100-page catalogue is devoted to his bequest.

Close neighbours were Arthur and Trudy Bliss at No 1 East Heath Road, a beautiful Georgian house with an amazing view over London. During Harold's frequent absences from home they would invite me round for a meal, or to show Arthur what I was working on at the moment. Indeed, it was he who was responsible for arranging the first performance of my Octet, three of whose four movements were written during 1932-33. When I played them to Arthur he said, 'Do you think you could get the work finished by November, for I'm involved then with some concerts at the Grotian Hall?' It was already June; but with the sublime optimism of youth I replied, 'Of course!', and straightway set off on a fortnight's walking-tour. In fact the work *was* finished by the 21st November, when the first performance was given by the Stratton String Quartet, Herbert Lodge, Frederick Thurston, Gilbert Vinter and Aubrey Thonger. Later the Octet was played, then recorded for Decca, by the Griller String Quartet, a remarkable group who met as students at the Royal Academy of Music and were to remain together for over 25 years. Their performance had totally unexpected consequences. A critique of the concert appeared in *The Times*, it was read by Ralph Hawkes, one of the directors of Boosey & Hawkes Ltd, and the firm thereafter became my publishers.

Among other works written at East Heath Road were my First Violin Sonata, introduced at the Wigmore Hall by Isolde Menges and Harold on 12 October 1932; *Three Medieval Carols*, broadcast by Dora Labette and myself in January 1934; the orchestral *Partita*, broadcast under Adrian Boult in June 1937; and the *Four Short Pieces* for clarinet and piano, played by my duo partner Pauline Juler at her Wigmore Hall recital on 12 October 1937.

As the *Partita* is published in two versions – for orchestra and for two pianos – I'm sometimes asked which came first. The answer, puzzlingly enough, is 'neither'. The work was first sketched in short score, then laid out for two pianos, and finally orchestrated. This explains a note on the title page, which reads, 'Each version was conceived for its own medium, so neither may be said to be an arrangement of the other'. The clarinet pieces (also published for viola and piano) were originally intended as simple piano solos using the white keys only – hence their modal flavour. Since my publisher showed little interest in these limitations, I later re-wrote them for piano and clarinet, an instrument I then happened to be learning.

The reason for taking up the clarinet so late in the day – I was then 26 – was to 'get the feel' of a wind instrument for the sake of composition. With considerable effrontery I wrote to Frederick Thurston, the wonderful clarinetist of the BBC Symphony Orchestra who had played in the first performance of my Octet, asking would he teach me? He kindly said Yes; and at our first lesson cheered me up by saying how nice it was to teach someone who could already *read* music. In the early days of practice the clarinet can make some fairly strange sounds. One day I was practising in my own room when Harold, walking upstairs with a friend, remarked perfectly seriously, 'I really *must* get that lavatory cistern seen to.' In the end, however, I was able to play the Beethoven Clarinet Trio, though not the more difficult Brahms works.

At about the same time I had begun to find my lack of German a great nuisance, for it cut me off from so much of interest that had been written about music. By a happy chance, Joy Finzi put me in touch with Mrs Hertha Kraft, a refugee from Nazi Germany, who now taught both privately and at a school in Kensington. She couldn't have been more helpful, and in a couple of years managed to instill in me a working knowledge of the language. After the grind of memorising irregular verbs and suchlike horrors, I found that reading German detective stories often suggested the meaning of an unfamiliar word, while German poetry gave the correct accentuation of the words themselves.

Two young musicians I met through Harold were Cedric Thorpe Davie and Benjamin Britten. Harold had awarded Cedric a prize at the Glasgow Musical Competitions, which led to his winning a Caird Scholarship and coming to London to study at the Royal Academy of Music. He was invited to tea at East Heath Road one day, we got to know one another, and thereafter remained lifelong friends. In his turn he introduced me to a much older friend of his at the Academy, Stuart Elliot. Stuart already had a medical degree, but studied piano and composition for the sheer pleasure of doing so. Later he concentrated on biochemistry, worked during the war at the Rockefeller Institute in New York, and eventually became a Fellow of Corpus Christi College in Cambridge. Indeed, I feel pretty sure that he was responsible for my much later removal to that delightful city. Cedric ended up as the Head of Music at the University of St Andrews in Scotland, surprisingly enough in succession to FH Sawyer, my old piano teacher in Belfast.

Britten was encountered in a more roundabout way. From the age of ten he had learnt the viola from Mrs Audrey Alston, who had been a fellow-student of Frank Bridge and Harold at the RCM, and now lived not far from Ben's home at Lowestoft in Suffolk. The eleven-year-old Ben was taken to the 1924 Norwich Festival, where he heard and was immensely impressed by Bridge's orchestral suite *The Sea*. Mrs Alston introduced him to Frank, who suggested that he should come up to London occasionally for a piano lesson with Harold. After one of these lessons I asked Ben to stay on for something to eat. But we weren't to meet for any length of time until 1935, when he phoned to say he had been asked to write film music for the GPO (later the Crown) Film Unit: would I be willing to come along and play the orchestral piano part? Never having done anything of the sort before I was delighted to say Yes; so a week later we went out to Blackheath, where the recording was to take place.

The music for his first film, *The King's Stamp*, was for two pianos (Ben and myself), flute, clarinet and percussion. For the next, *Coal Face*, the instrumental requirements were rather larger. They included me not only playing the piano, alone and in duet with Ben, but having to rattle iron chains and empty one bucket of water into another *rhythmically* – which is much more difficult than playing the piano.

A year later we recorded the still-famous *Night Mail*, with a brilliant spoken script by the poet Auden. This had to be synchronised exactly with the film, which Ben, as conductor, did perfectly.

We did not meet again until during the war, after Ben's return from America in 1942, when he and Peter Pears performed the *Seven Sonnets by Michelangelo* at the National Gallery Concerts, in which I was then involved. The songs were an enormous success and had to be repeated a few weeks later. Thereafter our paths crossed occasionally; but although I always admired Britten greatly as a musician, we were never close friends.

Much more important to me personally were the Warwick James family. Warwick himself was not only an eminent dentist (Harold and I were among his patients), but a distinguished Fellow of the Royal College of Surgeons who had performed many of the earliest facial reconstructions on wounded soldiers during the 1914 war. He was also an enthusiastic, if not very efficient, amateur cellist. His wife Mary, a warm-hearted West Country woman and former hospital nurse, made me feel a part of their large family of five sons and a daughter. They lived in Park Crescent, just south of Regent's Park, and latterly also had a house at Hurley, near Henley-on-Thames. I was invited there almost every weekend in summer to enjoy the country air, play tennis (the only game I enjoyed), and swim in the nearby Thames. Every year they gave a large party for their friends, in winter at Park Crescent or in summer at Hurley, and there Ivor James (also a patient, though no relation) and Harold played cello and piano sonatas and I played accompaniments for Ivor.

Another patient of Warwick's was TE Lawrence ('Lawrence of Arabia'), who, in his Aircrafthand's uniform, motorcycled up from Plymouth, where he was then engaged in testing high-speed motorboats. After his dental appointment he would be pressed to stay on to dinner, where, surprisingly short in stature, very silent, and with startlingly blue eyes, he merged unnoticed into the family. He was passionately keen on music; and when we still lived in Clarendon Road, Warwick would bring him to listen to us playing on two pianos. After he was killed in a motorcycle accident in 1935, we drove down to his cottage, Clouds Hill, on Egdon Heath, where the most striking objects among the sparse decorations were an EMG gramophone with a vast horn, and a white leather armchair-plus-reading-desk which he had designed for his own use.

Myra Hess had become a much-valued friend. Early in the century she and Irene Scharrer had been star pupils of Tobias Matthay (always known as Uncle Tobs) at the Royal Academy of Music. When she was 17, Myra made her début at the Queens Hall, playing solos and two concertos under the unlikely conductorship of young Mr Thomas Beecham. It was a great success. But in those days engagements for young pianists (particularly British ones) were few and far between, and for many years Myra had to support herself and her mother mainly by teaching. Irene was more fortunate. Being a wonderful natural Chopin player, and very good-looking into the bargain, her career soon outstripped Myra's. Almost inevitably, however, her loyalties became divided when she married an Eton housemaster (of all people) and had a family. Myra, on the other hand, remained single-mindedly faithful to the piano; and after an almost fortuitous success in Holland – she took the place of an indisposed pianist – her reputation was made.

A delightful surprise in the mid-1930s was to receive a poem from my friend Toty de Navarro, by then a well-known archaeologist and a Fellow of Trinity College, Cambridge. I say 'surprise' because at that time few people knew he wrote poetry – probably because he himself felt that much of it was essentially private. I was immensely impressed by the poem (now to be found on p57 of his *Collected Poems*), which contained a reference to Mozart's opera *Idomeneo*, of which we were both particularly fond. After this initial gift, Toty gave me a loose-leaf book containing typescripts of all the poems he wished to preserve; and thereafter sent me each new piece as it was written. Some fifteen months before his death in 1979 he went through all the poems with me, to settle not only the definitive version of each, but also the order in which they should appear. Finally he directed in his will that his widow Dorothy and I should prepare an edition of the works and have it privately printed. The result was *Collected Poems* by JM de Navarro, beautifully produced by The Rampant Lions Press of Cambridge in 1980. The originals were given to the Library of Trinity College, Cambridge, where they may be seen by arrangement with the Librarian.

A regular visitor from the North of Ireland to London was Mrs Jack MacIlwaine, mentioned earlier as a supporter of the Belfast Musical Competitions. I always used to visit her when on holiday in Belfast, play to her, and have endless talks about music. She was then the widow of a radiologist, had studied piano with Stavenhagen at the Royal Academy of Music, and was an ardent Wagnerite. She it was who gave me my first copy of *Der Ring des Niebelungen* – four rather tattered but greatly treasured volumes of the original Schott edition of the solo piano arrangement, with the German words printed above the staves. She came to London twice a year: once to take her niece to the latest plays, and once to take me to an orgy of German opera during the summer season at Covent Garden. As a result, I heard all the great Wagnerian singers of the day – such as Frieda Leider, Kirsten Flagstad (we heard her first London 'Isolde'), Maria Olczewska and Friedrich Schorr; and in non-Wagnerian roles, Elizabeth Schumann and Richard Meyer, the great Sophie and Baron Ochs in Richard Strauss's *Der Rosenkavalier*. On one memorable occasion we heard all these famous singers (also under Walter) 'letting their hair down' in the other Strauss's *Die Fledermaus*. It was quite unlike the usual performances one heard, and a wonderful demonstration of how the work *ought* to be sung and played. As a remembrance of these occasions I dedicated my orchestral *Four Diversions on Ulster Airs* 'To Mrs Mac.' The settings were originally written as part of a scheme, inaugurated by the Belfast BBC, to preserve the folksongs of Northern Ireland.

My father was also a regular visitor to London, when he was generally accompanied by my mother. His visits were primarily for meetings with the Directors of the Westminster Bank, to which his Ulster Bank was affiliated; but there was always time for theatres or other outings in the evening.

As I mentioned earlier, they were wonderfully helpful about my work. When our ancient Collard & Collard was superannuated, my father told me to hire a piano whenever I was on holiday in Belfast. Invariably it proved to be the twin of my little upright Bechstein in London, which made me feel thoroughly at home. Then, before my first public concerto appearance, without the slightest hint from me, my mother instinctively realised that I might not be feeling like a family dinner at that particular moment, so we went out for a quiet meal on our own.

In the spring of 1931 they decided to go on a Mediterranean cruise and take me with them – another advantage of being the youngest in the family. Our ship called at Lisbon, Malaga (where I first encountered the magical scent of freesias), Malta, Naples, Tunis and Algiers. On the outward trip the Bay of Biscay left me groaning in my cabin. But later the Mediterranean warmth was delightful, and everything else perfect until my poor father fell ill during the last few days of the trip, and had to be taken to a nursing-home in Southampton for a major operation. It was touch and go for some days; but in the end he weathered the crisis, and was able to convalesce at a pleasant hotel at Sandbanks near Bournemouth, where I visited them at weekends.

In 1936 Harold and I again had to move house because of the ending of our lease. This time it was left to me to look for a new home, for Harold had to go off on yet another of his overseas tours. I was lucky enough to find 34 Willoughby Road, a pleasant detached house in a quiet road, conveniently smaller than No 8 and only five minutes' walk away. It had an attractive music room on the first floor, and a sufficiently distant workroom-cum-bedroom for me, above the kitchen premises at the back of the house. No decorations were needed, so Pu, Betty and I were able to move in during March.

The year turned out to be fatally strenuous for Harold. From March until June he again travelled as one of the adjudicators at the Canadian National Competitive Festivals, giving some recitals in the United States betweenwhiles. On his return to England he was accompanied by young Randolph Hokanson from Seattle, who had been awarded a bursary to come and study with him. After only a month in London there was yet another South African tour. As it happened, my mother had been poorly for some time and had been advised to take a sea trip; so Harold suggested that we should accompany him as far as Cape

Town, and return by the next boat. (It was in the days before long-distance flights.) He stayed on for his tour, which as usual was very strenuous. It is scarcely surprising, therefore, that during his return voyage in November he had a severe coronary attack, and on arrival in Southampton was taken by ambulance straight to a nursing-home. (It seemed to me a fatal city.)

Warwick James and I immediately went down to Southampton, he to see that everything possible was being done for Harold, and I to stay there with him for the next six weeks.

As he appeared to be slowly improving, our faithful London doctor, Douglas Oakley, came down to Southampton with an ambulance to take him back to Willoughby Road. When he got there, poor Harold was completely disorientated, as he scarcely knew the house; and, to make matters worse, his bedroom had been moved to the downstairs dining-room in order to simplify nursing. In spite of the care of two nurses his condition began to deteriorate, and gradually it became apparent that he had had a secondary attack – probably when being removed from the boat – and that it had affected his brain. Everything possible was done to help him; but on 15 January 1937 Harold died, aged only 57. Though never a practising Jew, a Memorial Service was held for him three days later at the West London Synagogue.

Interlude III: Ashmansworth (1938)

After Harold's death I had little idea of what to do. I didn't want to go on living in 34 Willoughby Road, but hadn't enough money to lease another house in London at current prices. I looked at a small studio in Genilla Road, Hampstead, next door to one bought by Emmie Bass, but the owner wouldn't accept what I could offer for it.

A year later Gerald and Joy Finzi came to the rescue. There was an unoccupied gardener's cottage at the Ashmansworth site where they were building: why didn't Pu, Betty and I stay there until the new Church Farm was ready to receive them? It was a brilliant and generous suggestion.

As I didn't then have a car of my own, I rented the ancient Austin Seven belonging to William, the Finzis' gardener, who with his wife would eventually be occupying the cottage. In it we drove from London to Ashmansworth on 1 April 1938, a gloriously sunny day with the hedgerows covered in welcoming white blossom. The next day my Bechstein upright was delivered by Steinways to complete the household. It was a perfect way to spend eight or nine months: for besides the pleasure of being there, it gave me a chance of discovering whether I might like to build a small house in the country and live there permanently. In the end I decided No – probably because at heart I'm a townee, and at that time also found it both practical and stimulating to live in London.

Though already in the middle of writing my Piano Sonata in memory of Harold, I occasionally went up to London from Ashmansworth, either for professional work or to go to concerts. Outstanding among the latter were the six given by the BBC at Queen's Hall as The London Music Festival, three conducted by Koussevitsky and three by Toscanini. To add to the excitement they aroused, Adrian Boult – then Director of Music at the BBC and conductor of their orchestra – arranged for some of us to be allowed into rehearsals. Of these I particularly remember two things: first, in the Sibelius Seventh Symphony Koussevitsky used quadruple woodwind (instead of double), with the result that the important theme for flutes and bassoons just before letter Q could actually be heard; and second, that Toscanini – famed for his scrupulous adherence to the text – added violas to the divisi cellos at figure 9 in the first movement of Debussy's *La Mer*. Incidentally, at the beginning of the rehearsal of the second movement of the same work, when the downward swirl of the flutes was continually fluffed, he hurled down his baton and stormed off the platform. After five minutes of stunned orchestral silence, he was discreetly retrieved by Adrian Boult, and the rehearsal proceeded peacefully.

Short visits to London of this kind were all very well, but what was to be done about my longstanding acceptance of an invitation by Mrs Margaret Johnson, a former amateur pupil of Harold's, to take part in a two-car holiday in Germany and Austria for six weeks? With the Piano Sonata still unfinished, the Nazis rampant in Germany, and Austria recently annexed by Hitler, it scarcely seemed the right moment to visit either country. Yet had I not gone it could have put paid to the whole trip, which was to include Mrs Johnson's adopted daughter Primrose, and Randolph Hokanson, whom Mrs Johnson was now supporting. In the end, after much cogitation, I went.

Curiously enough, my most exciting experience during the whole trip was not musical, but the chance it gave me to see some woodcarvings by the great Bavarian sculptor Tilman Riemenschneider (1460-1531). I already knew that he had lived and worked in Würzburg from the age of 23, and had been Burgermeister of the city in 1520-21; but my first sight of his work was when we made a short stop at the village of Creglingen in Franken. There we visited the pilgrimage-church, which in those days was reached by a footpath over the fields. No wonder it is so famous. When you enter you are confronted by an enormous unstained limewood altarpiece of *The Life of the Virgin*, some 10 metres high, whose central figures are carved-in-the-round by Riemenschneider himself. The overall design is magnificent, while altogether typical of his work are the slender, sensitively carved hands, and the faces that must all be portraits of people he knew. (The sad-faced scribe in the predella is known to be the artist himself.)

We stayed the night in nearby Rothenburg-ob-der-Tauber, a beautiful mediaeval walled town where, in the Jacobskirche, we saw our second Riemenschneider, the Heiligenblutaltar depicting *The Last Supper*. Though exquisitely carved, it was a slight disappointment after

Creglingen, for at some stage it has been stained a dark mahogany-colour and is now badly worm-eaten.

Our main centre was to be Oberammergau in Bavaria, where Primrose had earlier worked in the Gasthaus of Anton Lang, a former Christus in the Passion Play. He was no longer alive; but the family – dear people who welcomed us warmly – still ran the Gasthaus.

We made one expedition to Munich to see *Don Giovanni* at the enchanting blue-and-gold Cuvilliés-Theater, bombed during the Second World War; and another to Salzburg for the Festival, where we saw *Fidelio* in the Festspielhaus, Goethe's *Egmont* (with Beethoven's music) in the Felsenreitschule, and heard Furtwängler conduct the Vienna Philharmonic in Bruckner's Seventh Symphony. (The English translation of the German programme-note described the slow movement as 'a deep deploration over the death of Wagner'!) Together with the excursions we made into the lovely surrounding countryside, it was an altogether fascinating experience – though horrifying to see shops with JÜDE daubed all over them and newly broken windows.

On our return to Oberammergau we nightly heard disquieting broadcasts from Nürnberg of the mad voice of Hitler haranguing the faithful, and threatening war on Great Britain and France if his territorial claims in the Sudetenland were not met. We would have returned to England immediately had it not been for an unfortunate mishap. The engine of one of our two cars broke down; and as the right make of spare part was not available in Germany, one had to be flown from England and fitted by a local garage. All this took time. Meanwhile my poor parents in Ireland must have been worrying their heads off. To set their minds at rest, I wired them to say that if the worst came to the worst we would abandon the ailing car, and make a dash in the remaining car for neutral Switzerland. In fact it didn't come to that. But I heaved a sigh of relief when, a few days later, we crossed with two cars into Holland at the border-town of Middleburg.

Back again in Ashmansworth I heard (with relief, I'm afraid) that Mr Chamberlain had visited Hitler in Berchtesgaden and returned to England with the wholly spurious promise of 'peace in our time'. From a purely selfish point of view, the shameful Munich Crisis had one advantage: it sent house prices in London plummeting.

Not long after my return I happened to see in the *Sunday Times*, under 'Properties for Sale', an advertisement for a house with studio in

Hampstead. This was exactly what I was looking for, so I hurried up to London to see the house-agents, Messrs Potter, only to be told that the house had already been sold. 'However', they added, 'we have for sale another house in Hampstead with a studio, would you care to see that?' When I discovered it was in Wildwood Road, where Myra Hess lived at No 48, I was even more excited. There and then they drove me to 106 Wildwood Road in the Hampstead Garden Suburb. It was a two-storied detached house on the corner of Meadway; and at the back (but attached to the house) there was a large single-storied music-room which had been added by the previous owner, a retired Borough Surveyor of Marylebone. (His wife was an amateur cellist, a pupil of Ivor James; and I always suspected the studio had been built in order to spare her husband the sound of practising.) After looking it over, inside and out, I decided that the house must be mine; and because of the international crisis I was able to buy a 70-year lease for the incredible sum of £2,600.

On our return from Germany, poor Primrose, Mrs Johnson's adopted daughter, had developed acute tuberculosis. To make matters worse, Mrs Johnson's few surviving relatives lived far off in the Potteries, so she had to cope with the terrible situation virtually on her own. I did what I could to help, but it was heartbreakingly little. After two months of agonising uncertainty, Primrose died.

At Wildwood Road the necessary re-decorations had been made, to enable Pu and Betty to move into our new house in December. I joined my parents in Belfast, as I had done for every vacation since schooldays. On my return to London in January 1939, I was walking across the Heath to Wildwood Road when, to my astonishment, the air-raid sirens began to wail. It must have been either a false alarm or a rehearsal; but it was a foretaste of things to come.

Chapter Four: 106 Wildwood Road
Pre-war and war years, 1939-1945

106 Wildwood Road was the ideal dwelling for our household. Beside 'the usual offices' there were three ground-floor rooms: a dining-room for formal occasions, a sitting-room for Pu and Betty, and the large single-storied studio which was my domain. Upstairs there were three bedrooms: a double room for Pu and Betty, a medium-sized spare room, and a much smaller dressing-room. Outside, a lawn and flower-beds edged three sides of the house, with a separate garage at one end. I'm not a gardener myself; but Betty was, and she delighted in looking after the plants that had been given us by the horticulturally knowledgeable Toty de Navarro.

The garage was soon occupied by a brand-new Morris Minor, a model that had recently come on the market. It was a thoughtful gift – a sort of non-wedding-present, from my mother's two unmarried sisters in Belfast, who must have astutely realised that I was unlikely to marry.

Though there were already built-in bookcases in several of the rooms, many more were required. In the dining-room I had a new set of shelves built to house art books and bound music such as the 45 volumes of the Bach-Gesellschaft and 10 volumes of Tudor Church Music. In the studio, under the large north-light window, a low cupboard with sliding doors held all the sheet music in labelled portfolios. It stretched across the width of the room, while opposite, between two smaller windows, were open shelves for miniature scores.

In a huge half-moon-shaped brick fireplace there was a 'Cozy Stove', which conveniently stayed alight all winter to keep me warm – central-heating was installed later; and on the other side of the room stood the inevitable Bechstein upright.

There was only one curious thing about the house itself. When we first moved in, I used the spare room as my bedroom; but I soon realised I couldn't possibly sleep there. I have no idea why. I'm not in the least a 'spooky' person, yet I knew that the spare room was not for me. Soon I moved to the much smaller dressing-room, and thereafter slept as soundly as could be wished.

The odd thing is that almost forty years later my pianist friend Stephen Kovasevich, who had bought the house, asked me whether I knew the place was haunted? When I asked why, he replied 'Because several of my guests have fled from the spare room in the middle of the night, complaining they couldn't remain there.' I must confess I've sometimes wondered whether this was due less to ghostly manifestations than to an attractive presence on the other side of the landing – but you never can tell.

There was only one disadvantage in living at No 106. As it is situated on the corner of Wildwood Road and Meadway, speeding motorists on both roads assume they have the right of way, with the result that collisions are apt to occur. It was not unusual to come downstairs in the morning and find a battered car sitting on the front lawn; and one New Year's Eve – perhaps the celebrations had something to do with it? – a car crashed through the hedge and landed with its bonnet wedged in the kitchen window. As my bedroom was just above, the police remarked reassuringly that it was lucky the car had a fibreglass body, otherwise my bed and I would have found ourselves on its roof.

One of the first things I noticed every night after I had gone to bed was that a remarkable whistler passed along the road. With the uninquiring habit of a Londoner, I never tried to find out who the whistler might be. Then one evening at a concert a friend happened to say to me, 'There's Gerard Hoffnung: you must meet him. He lives just beside you and he's mad on music.' 'Does he by any chance whistle?', I asked. 'Marvellously!' was the reply; and the mystery was solved. I had long known his enchanting cartoons, musical and otherwise, but had never realised that the plumpish, fresh-faced, bald young man I often saw walking on the Heath was Gerard.

When I got to know him I was astonished to discover that he couldn't read music. Having heard him whistle long stretches of many works with absolute accuracy, and dash off brilliant passages on his tiny saxophone or on one of his many ocarinas, it never occurred to me that all this might be done purely by ear. Yet when I offered him a score with which to follow a broadcast, he slowly answered, 'But, my dear fel-low, I can't *read* the thing!'

Later, when he had succumbed to his longing to possess a tuba, he used to appear on my doorstep, tuba tucked under his arm, with an apology for the interruption and the heartmelting request, 'How-ard, could you please make sure that I've got this piece right? I can manage the flats, but the sharps are im-*poss*-ible. He would then follow me into the house, sit down in front of a music-stand, and blow his way through a movement of the Tchaikovsky *Symphonie Pathétique*, while I interjected every now and again, 'No, Gerard, it's a sharp not a flat.'

At other times he would bring round a large envelope from which he extracted, one by one, the drawings for his next book of musical cartoons. These would be shown with an engaging mixture of uncertainty and suppressed delight, followed by an immense grin when, as invariably happened, they were greeted with roars of laughter.

As I wrote earlier, one of the great attractions of Wildwood Road was that Myra Hess was a near neighbour. She lived at No 48, a sunny, detached house that backed onto Highgate Golf Course and included a large music-room containing two Steinway grand pianos, one belonging to Myra herself, and the other on permanent loan from Steinways. In my early teens I had been introduced to her by Harold, who was an old friend; and after his death she in turn became a wonderful friend to me. Indeed – as will be seen later – she made me a part of her musical life.

Another musician friend was Isolde Menges. For many years she and Harold had a violin-and-piano duo partnership; and when he died she courageously asked me to take his place. I say 'courageously' because she was a long-established artist whereas I was little more than a beginner. Coming from a musical family, she had studied in St Petersburg and Berlin with Leopold Auer, and was well-known both in England and on the Continent. In spite of the difference in our ages and experience, we got along together extremely well, and I was to remain her pianist until she became mainly occupied with the Menges String Quartet.

As far as composition was concerned, since moving to Wildwood Road I concentrated on the Piano Sonata that had been begun before leaving Willoughby Road. Betweenwhiles were written Nos 2, 3 and 4 of the orchestral *Four Diversions on Ulster Airs*, mentioned earlier as being dedicated to my Irish friend 'Mrs Mac'. The three pieces were to be included in the 1940 Prom Concerts; but, like the Queen's Hall in which they would have been heard, that performance became a casualty of German bombers. Instead, the redoubtable Sir Henry Wood (never one to have his plans thwarted) gave the first performance during his Torquay Festival.

To return to 1939. As usual I went to Ireland for my summer holiday; but this time it was *un*usual in that I drove my mother and one of her unmarried sisters, my Aunt Ethel, for a trip to the west of Ireland, where I had never been before. Wonderful country – my father had prepared a splendid itinerary for us – and perfect weather throughout. Only one thing marred our enjoyment: in the middle of our tour we read of the German-Russian agreement, and realised that this meant war.

When we got back to Belfast I did my best to finish the Piano Sonata. Then, when war came on 3rd September with all its uncertainties, I wrote to R O asking him what I should do? He reassuringly replied, 'Stay where you are until you have to move.' Thus in spite of everything the Sonata was finished.

A month later Myra phoned excitedly from London to say she was planning a series of daily lunchtime concerts – these were the National Gallery Concerts (see Interlude IV) – they were to start on 10th October, and I must come over to London immediately to help her organise them. This was easier said than done, for it took time for a civilian to get a sailing permit in wartime. Eventually it was achieved, however, and though I always regret having missed the very first concert, I was there for the second and all the rest.

The National Gallery looked strange without its pictures – they had been removed for safety to a specially prepared mine in North Wales; but it was exciting to find that a platform had been erected beneath the Dome, that a Steinway concert-grand was sitting on it, and that the four radiating galleries were ready to receive audiences.

I constantly went up to Myra's house to help with the organisation, often driving her down to the Gallery in the little Austin Seven she had acquired in order to save petrol. For the first few months the Tuesday and Friday programmes were repeated at 4.30 in the afternoon, by which time it was of course dark. To comply with black-out regulations, headlights on cars were reduced to the merest slit, which didn't make for easy driving. On one occasion, Myra remarked encouragingly how well we were getting on just as I drove onto the pavement in Trafalgar Square.

Pu and Betty had meanwhile made the obligatory black-out curtains for Wildwood Road, where we had agreed that a draughty Anderson aid-raid shelter would *not* be installed in the back garden. Instead, an anti-blast brick wall was built just outside the dining-room French windows, our three beds were brought downstairs, and the ceiling was propped up by some rather frail-looking wooden supports. As air-raid precautions they were doubtless inadequate, but at least they enabled us to sleep surprisingly soundly through every subsequent night of the war. Not even the later arrival of an extremely noisy anti-aircraft gun emplacement on the nearby Heath Extension disturbed our slumbers, for we felt that we were at last receiving some protection.

One of the early casualties of the bombing was the block of flats lived in by Mrs Johnson, the hostess of our pre-war trip to Germany and Austria. Her drawing-room contained two Steinway grand pianos, one of which had been chosen for her by Harold when she had lessons from him. Luckily her furniture was not damaged; but of course she had to move. A flat was found in nearby Albert Road, with a pleasant view over Regent's Park; but alas its living-room was not large enough to accommodate two grand pianos. Most generously Mrs Johnson offered to give me the one chosen by Harold, I think in memory of both him and her daughter Primrose, who had died so tragically before the war. Needless to say, I was enormously grateful: not only for the gift itself, but also, in a curious way, because the Steinway would be joining the little Bechstein that Harold himself had given me so many years before. On its arrival at Wildwood Road it fitted snugly into the studio, where it was a very treasured possession.

The threads of concert-giving were gradually picked up, partly following the example of the Gallery concerts, and partly with the help of CEMA (The Council for the Encouragement of Music and the Arts). Musicians returned to their instruments and were only too happy to accept engagements whenever and wherever they turned up. Virtually the entire music profession appeared at the Gallery at one time or another, not least the younger performers, for whom it was the perfect venue for launching their careers. Two of the latter with whom I became closely associated were the pianist Denis Matthews and the violinist Yfrah Neaman. Denis's professor at the Royal Academy of Music, Harold Craxton, wrote to Myra saying that Denis would shortly be going into the RAF, and asking whether it would be possible for him to appear at the Gallery before doing so. As a result, Denis gave a joint recital with Maggie Teyte, and proved to be such a success that he was soon asked to appear on his own. Shortly after this, when the Brahms *Liebeslieder Waltzes* for four solo voices and piano-duet accompaniment were going to be performed, I asked Myra whether Denis and I might provide the accompaniment? (Incidentally, the ensemble was coached by Mrs Edward Speyer, the former Antonia Kufferath, who had given the first performance of a number of Brahms songs in the 1890s.) This proved to be the beginning of a partnership that lasted twenty-five years; for although there were then a number of two-piano teams, few of them played duets on *one* piano, which had greatly interested me ever since Harold introduced me to the repertoire in the 1920s.

Similarly, Yfrah's teacher, Max Rostal, asked whether Yfrah might be given a Gallery appearance. As a teenager he had won a Première Prix at the Paris Conservatoire, then studied privately with Jacques Thibault, luckily escaping to England after the fall of France. As an alien refugee he had been directed to work in a spectacles-factory; but Rostal, realising his potential, generously gave him free violin lessons betweenwhiles. For his first appearance at the Gallery he was partnered by Adela Kotowska, who regularly played for Rostal's pupils. For his second, Miss Kotowska fell ill at the last minute and I offered to take her place. Yfrah and I got on so well together that we decided to make it a permanent duo partnership; and this, like the one with Denis, lasted for twenty-five years, taking us as far afield as France, Holland, America, South Africa and India.

My other duo partnership, with the clarinettist Pauline Juler, continued to flourish; and at the Gallery, besides taking part in chamber music, I sometimes accompanied works of which I was particularly fond, such as Brahms's *Magelone Lieder*, Op 33, and *Daumer-Lieder*, Op 57, both with the tenor Jan van der Gucht, and Fauré's *La Bonne Chanson* with Sophie Wyss.

Among other musicians who became friends through the Concerts were the organist Geraint Jones and violinist Winifred Roberts, later to become his wife. An organist was required because it was preferable to have the continuo part in Bach Cantatas, and suchlike works, played on an organ rather than on the piano. At first this posed a problem; but it was solved when Messrs Boosey & Hawkes generously lent us a

Hammond electronic organ, which took its place inconspicuously on the platform beside the Steinway. It may not have provided the ideal organ sound, but it fulfilled its purpose and was duly appreciated. As well as playing for us at the Gallery, Geraint gave a remarkable series of recitals at a London church, at which he played the complete organ works of Bach – Myra and I often went to them. He also introduced me to Thurston Dart, who, as will be seen later, played an important part in my own musical life. Originally a mathematician, he was primarily a remarkable musician, who after the war became successively Lecturer in Music at Cambridge, Professor there, and at King's College, London.

At the beginning of the war the BBC moved its Orchestra and Music Department to Bristol, oblivious of the fact that that city would eventually receive its share of bombs. Studios were improvised in church halls and office blocks all over the town, performers were given a rail ticket to Bristol and thereafter left to their own devices. No one met them at Temple Meads station or guided them to the studio concerned – at least, not until the eminent harpist Maria Korchinska was seen pushing her instrument studio-wards on a station trolley.

Travelling to engagements, wherever they happened to be, was not always easy, for trains were invariably overcrowded and carriages necessarily ill-lit. Once, after giving a concert in Bridlington with the Griller Quartet, the five of us had to stand in the guard's van all the way from York to London. After the devastating raids on Bristol the BBC Orchestra was moved to Bedford, while other departments were scattered over the countryside. The South American Service found itself in a Victorian mansion several miles from Evesham in Worcestershire. Performers were housed for the night in an Evesham hotel, awakened at 3 am, and driven out to the studio to fulfil their engagement – all because of the time-difference between the two countries, and the fact that wartime broadcasts *had* to go out live.

Like everyone else, I was eventually caught up in the war machine. Unlike most, however, I was lucky enough to enter the RAF with the Griller Quartet. Some years before war broke out, Sir Walford Davies, the Master of the King's Music, had suggested to the Air Ministry that musicians might contribute more to a war-effort as musicians rather than as inefficient aircraftsmen. Surprisingly enough, the Air Ministry agreed. Thus when the time came, members of string quartets and other musicians were drafted to Uxbridge, where the RAF Band was stationed, in order to turn it into the RAF Orchestra. In command was Wing-Commander Peter O'Donnell, who, though doubtless an excellent band-master, was no conductor of classical music. Known as 'Two-gun Pete', from his habit of directing the orchestra with extended forefingers rather than a baton, he was said to learn the Beethoven Symphonies from borrowed gramophone records. Nevertheless, he was sympathetic to the musicians under his control, and was generally willing to give them the permission needed to accept outside engagements, without which public music-making would have come to a halt.

While at Uxbridge I met Tim Scott, who was in the RAF Photographic Interpretation Unit at Medmenham, and had become a friend of the Griller Quartet during one of their visits there. Throughout his later postings we kept in touch by means of that invaluable wartime invention the air-letter, which, to save space, micro-filmed one's missives and forwarded them to their destination by air. After the war he worked abroad for the British Council, and on his retirement became a professional antiquarian book-seller. He now carries on the business from an attractive house in Lewes, Sussex, which he shares with his Gurkha friend Pasang Tamang, and where I often stay with them for visits to the opera at nearby Glyndebourne.

For more than one of us, Friday 30 August 1940 was specially memorable. At the Proms, Myra gave her first performance of the *Emperor Concerto*; Toty de Navarro came up to London to hear it and stayed with us at Wildwood Road, and the Griller Quartet and I entered the RAF.

After hearing Myra's *Emperor* at Queen's Hall, Toty returned to Wildwood Road, and for some reason took a powerful sleeping-draught before going to bed. In the middle of the night Pu and Betty were horrified to hear approaching bombers. They rushed upstairs to the spare room, where they had the greatest difficulty in rousing Toty and convincing him that it would be safer to come downstairs. Meanwhile the Grillers and I, on night-time guard-duty at Uxbridge, saw the terrible glow in the sky above the docks in the East End of London, which, after the sporadic bombing of the 'phoney war', signalled all too clearly the beginning of the real 'blitz'.

An important advantage of being at Uxbridge was that we were only required for duty (i.e. rehearsals) during the morning, which left us free to return home in the afternoon and sleep there at night. The journey between Wildwood Road and Uxbridge was no problem, since my car, which had been laid-up in the garage since the beginning of the war, could now be re-floated, as it were, on the petrol coupons that were provided for those on 'official duty'. Thus I could continue to help Myra with Gallery work in the afternoons and evenings, and often get down to the concerts themselves.

One of the delights of our work together was when the orchestral part of a concerto had to be supplied on the second piano at No 48. This was mainly during the period when Myra was studying the twenty-one concertos of Mozart, for although a number of them were already in her repertoire, others had to be learnt from scratch.

The only people invited to these sessions were Sir Stafford Cripps and his wife Isobel – he for the relaxation it afforded from his arduous work as Chancellor of the Exchequer, and both of them for their friendship with Myra. At that time his public image was of a dour, unrelenting disciplinarian, mainly, I think, because of his thankless task as Chancellor. But in fact he was a man of great warmth with a totally unexpected sense of humour. (One of his favourite gramophone records was 'The Village Concert', in which the various items were introduced in an unctuous, clerical voice by Sidney Howard.) Before becoming Chancellor he had been the British Ambassador in Moscow, whence his faithful butler sent him tins of caviar throughout the war. As both Sir Stafford and Lady Cripps were vegetarians, these kindly gifts were not really appreciated. But as they were generally passed on to Myra, she and I enjoyed many an unexpected caviar feast, at which her one complaint would be, 'If only we could have just a *tiny* squeeze of lemon juice!'

Though I could still fit in piano practice, composition was too time-consuming. In fact the only music I wrote during the war was the set of *Five Bagatelles* for piano, which arose in a curious way. Getting tired of having written nothing for so many years, I said to a friend one day, 'I'm sure I could write something if only someone would give me a few notes to start on.' 'Here they are', he replied, and scribbled on the back of an envelope the six rather unlikely notes that form the theme of Bagatelle No 2. The piece was duly written, and proved so agreeable – to me, at least – that I asked for some more notes. These were supplied, and turned out to be the basis of the *Bagatelles*, and also the reason for their dedication 'to Arnold van Wyk, who kindly contributed twenty-five notes'.

Despite blitzes day and night, and the later V-Ones (pilotless bombs) and V-Twos (enormous rockets), the Gallery concerts continued without a break. When their fifth anniversary came in view we felt it should be commemorated in some way; so we put together a 76-page booklet which was published by the National Gallery on 10 October 1944. It consisted mainly of a list – 50 pages long – of the works that had been performed, and another of their performers. It also included messages from Myra and Sir Kenneth Clark (the Director of the Gallery), and a history of the concerts themselves. It was felt there should be a contribution from a non-musician, and when I boldly suggested E M Forster, Myra asked, 'Do you know him?' I replied, 'No, but he often comes to the concerts.' 'Then let's ask him to lunch!' said Myra. And so it was that after one of the concerts he lunched with us at the Garrick, a favourite pub just round the corner, and nobly said he would be delighted to accept our rather preposterous suggestion. The result was the typically witty little essay 'From the Audience',. which provided exactly the light touch required.

Another unlikely encounter involved the founding of the Courtauld Music Trust. Myra had long admired the young Griller String Quartet, and had even given a fillip to their debut New York recital by joining them in a piano quintet; she also often appeared with them at the Gallery concerts. She was worried, however, about their precarious finances. Most unfairly, quartets do *not* receive a fee four times larger than that of a soloist; and as the Grillers had made it a rule never to appear otherwise than as a quartet, they could not increase their earnings either by playing in orchestras or by appearing individually. Myra asked me one day whether I could think of any way out of the difficulty – perhaps a wealthy music lover might be willing to support them? I immediately said that the obvious person was Mr Samuel Courtauld, head of Courtaulds Ltd, the makers of artificial silk. He was well-known as an art lover, had founded the Courtauld Institute for Art Studies, and his wife, before she died, had financed the pre-war Courtauld-Sargent Concerts. With memories of our success with E M Forster, Myra suggested inviting him to lunch, though neither of us knew him. At a restaurant rather more elegant than the dear old Garrick, we explained the problem to him. He was most sympathetic, and particularly interested in the idea since the Grillers had played more than once at musical parties at his house in South Audley Street. He told us that Mrs Courtauld had left a considerable sum specifically for musical purposes; and though some of it had already been earmarked, he would like to found a Trust Fund in her memory with the rest. Provided, that is to say, that I would be its secretary, and look after the details of its setting-up! Seeing that I was rather startled by this suggestion, he added that of course he would put me in touch with his solicitors, who would look after all technical matters. An admirable Deed of Trust was drawn up by Sir Steuart Wilson, later Head of the Arts Council, which at Mr Courtauld's own suggestion widened the scope of the trust to include musicians other than the Grillers. The beneficiaries remained the Griller Quartet until finally they settled at the University of California in Berkeley, USA. Thereafter, other young musicians were helped either with the purchase of instruments, fees for lessons, or other necessary objects.

At last the war in Europe came to an end on Tuesday 8 May 1945; but strangely enough it was not quite the end of the Gallery Concerts. There was considerable controversy as to whether they should continue indefinitely (see Interlude IV); but finally, in a truly British compromise, they were allowed to go on for a further six months. Thus, to the disappointment of many and the satisfaction of some, the National Gallery Concerts came to an end on Wednesday, 10 April 1946.

Interlude IV: The National Gallery Concerts

If Myra Hess had been asked what was the most remarkable episode in her life, there is little doubt that she would have replied 'The National Gallery Concerts'. In order to understand this, two facts must be borne in mind: first, when war was declared on 3 September 1939, Myra immediately cancelled an extensive American tour, feeling that her place was in her own country, even if at the moment she had little idea what she could do there. And second, all theatres, cinemas and concert halls in London had been closed by order of the Home Office; museums and galleries were emptied of their treasures, and Londoners were left, in the intervals of putting up black-out curtains and evacuating children, to meditate on their possible fate. Though such restrictions were doubtless necessary in the initial emergency, they could not remain in force indefinitely, for people required mental and spiritual stimulus as well as food. No one felt this more strongly than Myra, who became increasingly convinced that countless people were being starved of serious music – the BBC ground out cinema-organ music all day long – and that she must try to do something about it.

While spending a late-September weekend in Surrey with her old teacher Tobias Matthay, she spoke of this and asked the other members of the party whether they thought it might be possible to arrange some concerts? If so, where could they be given?

'Why not in the National Gallery?' asked her optimistic friend Denise Lassimone.

'Why not in Buckingham Palace?' replied the less sanguine Myra.

Yet surprisingly enough, Denise's unlikely idea bore fruit. The Director of the National Gallery, Sir Kenneth Clark, was approached and enthusiastically agreed that since pictures could no longer be seen there, it was wholly appropriate that music should be heard instead. Permission to hold the concerts was obtained from the Trustees of the Gallery and the Office of Works; and the Home Office agreed to relax its ban forbidding crowds to gather in public buildings. It was then announced in the press and on radio that a series of lunchtime concerts of chamber music would take place in the National Gallery from

Mondays to Fridays at 1 pm, with a repeat of the Tuesday and Friday programmes at 4.30 (these afternoon concerts were discontinued after two-and-a-half months) Admission would be one shilling (the equivalent of today's 5p), and any profits would go to the Musicians' Benevolent Fund, for the profession had been hard hit by the cessation of concert-giving throughout the country.

Five days later, on Tuesday 10 October 1939, Myra herself gave the first concert – 'in case the whole thing is a flop', as she put it. She needn't have worried. Long before the doors opened, a line of people stretched down the steps of the Gallery and round the far corner of Trafalgar Square; and by the time the doors had to be closed on the disappointed tail-end of the queue, roughly a thousand people had crowded into the Gallery. (The Home Office had given permission for an audience of 200.) More than half had to stand; but all listened entranced to a programme of Scarlatti, Bach, Beethoven, Schubert, Chopin and Brahms; and from that moment Myra's dream of providing music daily for whoever wished to hear it became a practical reality.

No one had expected such an overwhelming response. Thinking that only a few dozen of her friends might turn up, Myra had asked Beryl Davis, her niece and wartime secretary, to take the money at the door. When the flood of people poured in, poor Beryl found she had no change for the first person in the queue, who happened to present a half-crown for his shilling ticket. The concerts had started with literally nothing in the till.

The continued success of such a venture depended, of course, on the goodwill and co-operation of the entire music profession. This never failed. Every artist, from the most famous to the youngest recruit, came for a flat-rate token fee in recognition of the fact that they were helping a splendid cause. And Myra felt that she could ask this of her colleagues, not only because she herself accepted nothing whatever for any work connected with the concerts, but also because artists were only booked a few weeks in advance, so that an appearance at the Gallery never meant the loss of a more lucrative engagement.

From the outset Myra's aim had been twofold: to present first-rate chamber music at a price all could afford, and to give young and promising performers an opportunity of appearing before a ready-made audience, side by side with already established artists. Chamber music of every kind, instrumental and vocal, plus a certain amount of music for small orchestra, constituted the hour-long programmes. Sometimes they were devoted to works by a single composer – oddly enough these always drew a larger audience than a mixed programme – the most popular being Beethoven, Mozart and Bach, in that order. Various series were given from time to time, such as the complete chamber works of Beethoven or Brahms; the Bach 48 Preludes and Fugues and *Brandenburg Concertos*; and the twenty-one Mozart Piano Concertos, played by Myra herself.

Programmes were planned about a month in advance by Myra and myself. (When the concerts finally came to an end she said to me, 'Isn't it extraordinary, Howardy? We've worked together for six-and-a-half years without actually hitting one another!') They were then passed on to Messrs Ibbs & Tillett, the concert agents, who booked the artists for us and made all the arrangements for printing and advertising. Weekly programmes were on sale at the Gallery and elsewhere – they became smaller and smaller as the paper shortage grew more acute – while detailed programmes were available for each day's concert. These and statistical records of every aspect of the concerts were carefully kept by Beryl Davis; and as they formed a uniquely comprehensive view of the whole scheme, they were eventually bound up in a series of volumes and bequeathed by Myra to the British Library.

Audiences varied between 200 and 1,750 daily, depending on such factors as the war news, the weather, the type of programme offered (a solo pianist drew more than a string quartet, and a singer less than either), the eminence of the performer, and even the day of the week.

Smooth organisation was not achieved in a day, nor was it maintained without incident through the vicissitudes of war. But eventually the concerts could make the proud boast, in company with the famous girlie-show at the Windmill Theatre, that they had never once closed down.

The daylight air-raids of the Battle of Britain made it necessary, in September 1940, to move the concerts from the glass-roofed Dome to the downstairs Shelter-room, where greater safety was to be found at the expense of comfort and space. With intensive night-raids of the winter of 1940-41 difficulties increased daily. Audiences and performers alike would pick their way through glass-strewn streets flanked by smouldering buildings, to find the Gallery miraculously still standing, though scarred and without heating of any kind. The Shelter, which in September had seemed so airless, developed an unbelievable number of piercing draughts; and large pools of water collected on the floor, in spite of the tireless efforts of the faithful Mr Smith, the wartime Head Attendant at the Gallery. The cold became intense. Performers battled with blue fingers, helped only by a couple of oil-stoves on the platform, while audiences wrapped themselves in rugs and top coats.

At 11 o'clock on the morning of 15 October 1940, Myra was told on the phone that a time-bomb had fallen on the Gallery and that the building must be evacuated immediately. Half an hour later the High Commissioner for South Africa had generously placed at our disposal the Library in nearby South Africa House; so, time-bomb or no, that day's concert took place, and, for the only occasion, outside the National Gallery. On returning to the Gallery another time-bomb was found in the wreckage; so the concerts were hurriedly moved to a room in the most distant part of the building. A couple of days later, in the middle of a Beethoven String Quartet, the bomb went off with a terrific explosion. By a miracle nobody was hurt; and as the Shelter escaped with only broken windows, the concerts were able to return there once more.

With the decrease in air-raids it became possible in June 1941 to move the concerts back to their original home under the Dome. It was a double relief, for the nine months of restricted accommodation in the Shelter, and the consequently diminished audiences, had put a severe strain on financial resources. Indeed, it is not at all certain that the concerts could have continued had it not been for a timely gift of £4,000 from the United States. This splendid sum was contributed by Myra's countless American friends and admirers as a token of appreciation for all that she had done and was doing for music and her country.

After their return to the Dome the concerts continued with unabated success, and without further interruption until the flying-bomb attacks in the summer of 1944 made a temporary return to the Shelter advisable. Luckily this lasted only three months, as the Gallery escaped damage both then and during the later rocket attacks.

With the beginning of the liberation of Europe came the first intoxicating visits of performers from abroad. Francis Poulenc and

Pierre Bernac were the earliest to arrive, bringing with them an unknown young violinist called Ginette Neveu, whose masterly playing made a profound impression on all who heard her. Nor was the traffic in one direction only. Myra herself was invited to return to Holland even before the fighting there had finished; to be greeted by the Dutch not only as a beloved long-lost friend, but also as a near-miraculous proof of their country's ever-growing freedom.

This period also brought its problems. As the foreseeable end of the war in Europe drew nearer, Myra became increasingly concerned about the future of the concerts. She was perfectly willing to accept the partial sacrifice of the rest of her career, provided the trustees of the Gallery agreed to the concerts continuing there indefinitely. A memorandum outlining a possible scheme was forwarded to the trustees by Sir Kenneth Clark with his blessing, though he himself would soon be leaving the Gallery. As a result, it was agreed that the concerts should continue in the Dome for another year at least, and that the position should then be reviewed.

This renewed proof of the Trustees' appreciation was encouraging. But as peace came to Europe and 1945 drew to a close, Myra felt she would soon have to know one way or the other about the future, for America was clamouring for her long-postponed return and could not be expected to wait indefinitely for a yes or a no. At the beginning of 1946 she asked the Chairman of the Trustees, Mr Vincent Massey, for a firm decision. On 14 February, while in Oxford to give a recital, she heard by phone that the Trustees had decided it was not going to be possible to continue the concerts because of the reconstruction work that was planned for restoring the building. It was a bitter blow.

The date chosen for the final programme was 10 April 1946, which meant that the concerts had run without a break for exactly six-and-a-half years. At it the Griller String Quartet rounded off their many appearances at the Gallery by playing works by Haydn and Beethoven – surely an appropriate way to bring the concerts to a close, for a string quartet is the most perfect form of chamber music, and chamber music was what Myra had so long ago determined to provide.

Thus an extraordinary and imaginative adventure came to an end. In all, 1,698 concerts had been given, in which the number of performers taking part totalled 238 different pianists, 236 string players, 64 wind players, 157 singers, 24 string quartets and 56 other ensembles, besides

13 orchestras, 15 choirs, and 24 conductors. Over £23,000 had been paid in artists' fees; more than £16,000 had been contributed to the Musicians' Benevolent Fund; and over three-quarters-of-a-million people had come to listen to chamber music. The exact total was 824,152.

Chapter Five: 106 Wildwood Road
Post-war years, 1945–1972

When the National Gallery Concerts came to an end in April 1946 I realised that something drastic must be done if I was to resume serious composition; so I told most of my friends that I was going away for some months to write. In fact I stayed comfortably at home in Wildwood Road, while dear Pu helpfully, if untruthfully, parried all phone calls. The only two friends who knew where I was were Gerald Finzi and Myra. She, with her usual tact, made no demands whatever. But what was my alarm when, walking along Oxford Street one day, I saw Gerald approaching. I needn't have worried. Like a true friend he passed by silently, with no more than a conspiratorial wink to show that he was quite aware of what was afoot.

During these several months 'in purdah' I managed to produce my Second Violin Sonata. I immensely enjoyed working on it, but was faintly surprised that the three movements were written in the reverse order, ie, 3, 2, 1.

Shortly after 'emerging' I was invited by Sir Stanley Marchant, the Principal of the Royal Academy of Music, to do some composition teaching there. I said I'd be delighted to do so, provided it didn't involve teaching either harmony or counterpoint, which I felt I wouldn't be very good at. Sir Stanley helpfully agreed to this proviso; and as a result I taught composition (as far as one can do so) at the RAM one day a week for the next fifteen years.

Particularly interesting were the three friends Richard Rodney Bennett, Susan Bradshaw and Cornelius Cardew. By a curious coincidence, Richard's mother had been one of Harold's piano pupils at the RCM. And though I hadn't seen her for many years, she wrote to ask whether I thought Richard could make a financial success of composition. I replied that he was the only person I had ever met about whom I had no doubts whatever on that score. He seemed able to do anything and everything. Susan was extremely gifted, yet oddly distrustful of what she wrote – I think I saw only one of her completed compositions, so we generally passed the time by playing piano duets.

Cornelius, when he first came, was wholly under the influence of his uncle Phil, a well-known writer of light music. My aim to lead Cor into more interesting paths was all too successful, for by the time he left me I couldn't understand a thing he wrote. He and Richard used to play Boulez's *Structures* for two pianos, apparently with complete accuracy; the only problem being that I never knew when the pages should be turned.

While teaching at the RAM I met Richard Butt, who, though not a pupil, became a close friend. He was then studying violin but later became a music administrator, first in successively Leicester and Norwich, and eventually as Head of Music at the BBC in Birmingham. In later years I often visited him and his friend Stanley Sellers, generally to go to one of the Welsh National Opera performances in Birmingham, or to the Shakespeare Theatre in Stratford, which was only half an hour away. We also used to go off on what we called 'church crawls' to inspect interesting old churches, sometimes as far afield as Yorkshire or Herefordshire. The latter interested me particularly, ever since I first encountered the Herefordshire-Romanesque school of sculptors at Kilpeck Church, South of Hereford. It must have consisted of one extremely gifted Master and a small group of followers, who worked almost exclusively in a dozen churches strung along the English-Welsh border. We were so impressed by their work that we later took our friend Nigel Luckhurst, a professional photographer from Cambridge, to record all twelve churches, and eventually held an exhibition of his photographs at the Three Choirs Festival at Hereford in 1991.

With the ending of the war in 1945 it once again became possible to go abroad for professional engagements. The first that Yfrah and I accepted were broadcasts from Paris and Hilversum in 1947. The problem about foreign travel then was that one had to pay in England for all one's travel and hotel expenses. Only the equivalent of £5 could be taken out of England in cash; otherwise it was travellers' cheques. As we had to change trains in Brussels on our way from France to Holland, I told Yfrah that we must find time to have lunch at the marvellous Restaurant Royale there, to which Harold had taken me before the war. Cosily seated in its Edwardian splendour we enjoyed starters, a bottle of wine (of course), and wonderful beef steaks the like of which we hadn't seen for seven years. When Yfrah asked what sweet we should have to round off the meal, I suggested that it might be wise first to tot up the bill. Sure enough, we found we didn't have enough to pay for what we had already consumed; so Yfrah hurriedly went to the nearest Thomas Cook to cash some more travellers' cheques. When the bill was finally settled – without any sweets – we found there wasn't enough left to pay for a taxi back to the station. Instead, we ignominiously took a tram; and, staggering under the weight of our luggage, limped along platforms and across footbridges until, exhausted, we collapsed into our elegant (but of course pre-booked) first-class carriage.

On my summer holiday to Belfast in 1948 I decided to write a ballet. It was based on 'The Nun's Priest's Tale' from Chaucer's *Canterbury Tales*, and was called *Chauntecleer*. I had enormous fun planning, writing and scoring it; but on mature consideration I decided the music wasn't up to scratch, so withdrew it. Besides, a ballet about hens wasn't very practical.

A year later just the right stimulus was provided when the Council for the Encouragement of Music and the Arts of Northern Ireland invited me to write a Piano Concerto for the Festival of Britain. It turned out to be for piano and string orchestra, and I myself gave the first performance in the Ulster Hall on 22 June 1951. A year later the first performance in England was given by Myra Hess at the Royal Festival Hall, and in America the year after that at Carnegie Hall in New York. At the rehearsal in Carnegie I had the totally unexpected pleasure of re-meeting Stuart Elliot, whom I hadn't seen for years. He was working at the Rockefeller Institute (later University), and had read an announcement of the concert in the press. We met frequently thereafter, not only in New York, but later when we had both returned to England.

1951 seemed to be a good year for commissions, for I was next asked for some songs, to be included in a recital given by Monica Sinclair and John Gardner at Morley College in London. The words I chose were five poems by Denton Welch, whose prose I greatly admired. The cycle is called *Discovery*, after the title of the final song. I don't think Welch's poetry is nearly as good as his prose; yet in a curious way it's just right for setting: for its very incompleteness always leaves something for the music to say.

Another commission from CEMA was for an orchestral work to celebrate the Coronation of Queen Elizabeth II in 1953. This was the *Overture for an Occasion*, which seeks to combine the expected jollifications with some more serious thoughts.

Uncommissioned were the *Five Irish Folksongs* which I set for voice and piano. Both words and melodies come from the Sam Henry Collection, which had already provided the basis of the orchestral *Four Diversions* of 1940-42. About the vocal set there are two notable facts. The third song, 'Calen-O', was well known at the time of Shakespeare, for it is referred to in *Henry V*, and appears in the *Fitzwilliam Virginal Book* in a keyboard setting by William Byrd. The fourth song, 'The Swan', must originally have been in 4/4 time (not 3/4). Sam Henry was an exciseman, not a professional musician, and unfamiliar with normal musical notation. As he wrote down the many songs he collected in tonic sol-fa, the results are sometimes rather unexpected. Though 'The Swan' should undoubtedly be in 4/4, I kept to Henry's incorrect 3/4 as I found it more interesting.

After our initial foray to France and Holland, Yfrah and I made a number of professional trips abroad: to Israel in 1951, India in 1954, and several times to South Africa, which always included a month for me to stay with my friend Arnold van Wyk. Perhaps the most unexpected was India, where we were engaged to make a tour by a mainly Parsee group called the Bombay Madrigal Singers (one imagined them carolling William Byrd and Orlando Gibbons). At a recital in Karachi I was confronted by one of those awful little baby grands, so small that one is never sure where the keyboard is lurking. Then, for a concert with the Calcutta Symphony Orchestra, we had to rehearse our concertos at 8 am, because the players were occupied with other work during the day. We were put up by the obviously very wealthy amateur conductor, whose grand house contained everything except books. After the concert he and his wife entertained us at a smart night-club, which was perhaps not the best follow-up to Beethoven.

The trouble about tours in interesting countries is that there is never sufficient time to see the things you really want to see. One evening we had arranged to visit the Taj Mahal by moonlight. Instead, we had to attend a reception at which the food was undoubtedly marvellous, but the drinks were pink and strictly non-alcoholic.

Harold Samuel, c.1923
(see Interlude I, page 16)

Gerald Finzi, c.1940
pencil drawing by Joy Finzi
(see Interlude II, page 29)

Ashmansworth (1938); the gardener's cottage. The conservatory has been added since our day.

The National Gallery Concerts, the first audience, 10 October 1939 (see Interlude IV, page 57)

Arnold van Wyk (1946) at the BBC (see Interlude V, page 82)

On the way back from India we stopped in Athens to give a recital at the British Council, where Francis King entertained us to delicious meals and all the local gossip. Then, at my request, we spent a couple of days in Istanbul, where I was anxious to see the mosaics in Santa Sophia. In fact they were slightly disappointing; but the inside of the building itself is one of the most impressive I have ever seen. It was well worth the stop-over. The only difficulty was that my bank in London had omitted to make our travellers' cheques valid in Turkey. As we hadn't a penny of Turkish currency we had to throw ourselves on the mercy of the British Council, who are usually so good in such emergencies. The Scottish director took us out to lunch; but when it came to hard cash he was less helpful. We had the greatest difficulty in extracting from him our hotel expenses; and when I asked how they should be repaid, he quoted the official rate of exchange, though he had told us earlier that he always changed his money on the more advantageous black market.

On returning home I found that my dear Pu was slowly fading away. She was looked after at Wildwood Road by Betty and a sister of Betty's, who was a hospital nurse and happened to be working in a nearby nursing-home. Pu had been with me very nearly continuously since I was one month old, so the loss was heart-breaking. Yet, in a curious way, it was a comfort to know that at the age of 80 she had died under my own roof. I told Betty afterwards that she must feel free to return to Ireland if she so wished. But No: she had been with me for 30 years and would like to stay on.

Only six years later Betty herself died under circumstances that were never explained. One night I was fast asleep when, at about midnight, there was a tap on my door – something that had never happened before. It was Betty, to say that she was feeling very unwell. I told her to go back to bed, and that I would phone for the doctor. When I went in to her room to see her comfortably settled, I was horrified to notice a trail of blood along the floor. Worse still, her bed was soaked in blood. I immediately phoned 999 for an ambulance, and as soon as it arrived Betty was carried down on a stretcher. But alas, by the time they got her to hospital she was dead.

Two policemen then arrived at Wildwood Road (they must have been notified of the 999 call), and began questioning me about what had happened. When I asked could I go and begin to clear up the mess, they said No, they wanted to look round for a bit. They then went up to the bedroom, obviously to look for the 'sharp instrument' with which someone could have murdered Betty (perhaps me?). After half an hour's fruitless search they departed, saying that I could now clear up.

To add to the horror, another sister of Betty's was arriving from South America with her husband the following morning. I phoned Heathrow asking that the husband should phone me as soon as they landed. He did so, and I broke the news to him as best I could. Later, of course, there had to be an inquest, to which I was not bidden. But the extraordinary thing is that Betty's sister – who herself had been a hospital nurse – was never told, nor could she find out, in spite of repeated enquiries, how her sister had died.

On one of my many visits to Broadway after Toty's marriage to Dorothy Hoare, a former Fellow of Newnham College, Stephen Kovasevitch, the young American pianist, came to give an afternoon recital. When he arrived in his car he asked if he might bring in a friend who had come with him from London. The friend turned out to be Jacqueline du Pré, who was of course warmly welcomed. Jackie was the brilliant young cellist who had given her debut recital at Wigmore Hall at the age of 17. For several years she and Steve played sonatas together in the days before she met and married Daniel Barenboim.

After Steve's recital they were invited to stay on to dinner. At the end of the meal Steve mentioned casually that there happened to be a cello in the car (it was of course Jackie's Strad), might they bring it in and play some sonatas to us? Thus it came about that the four of us – the two Navarros, Gertrude Caton Thompson (the archaeologist), an old friend of theirs, and myself – spent a never-to-be-forgotten evening listening to the D major Sonatas of Bach and Beethoven.

The heartbreaking thing for all her friends and admirers was that in 1973 Jackie was found to be suffering from multiple sclerosis. After 14 years of increasing debility she died at the age of 42.

Among many continental holidays that were not concert tours, several were specially memorable. In 1956 Hilda Dederich, a pianist and an old friend of Myra's, invited me to visit her villa overlooking Lake Maggiore. Before the war, when she was staying at Cecil Lewis's house beside the lake, he happened to mention that the plot beside his own was for sale, and she should buy it. The friendly local mayor,

Adolfo, would build her a house out of the rock blasted from her own land, the furniture (except for comfortable beds) would be made locally, and she could come out to it three times a year during the RAM holidays. Hillie fell for his suggestion. It was a blissful place, 200 feet above the lake, with an uninterrupted view of Stresa on the far shore. Hillie was the perfect hostess, always ready to take one out for a lovely drive, to play Scrabble, and to provide the delicious meals cooked by Anna, her daily help from the village.

After a week of sybaritic living – breakfast in bed every morning – I set off for Florence, where I had always wanted to go. I could hardly believe I was there and actually able to see the paintings and sculpture I had previously known only through reproductions in books. Overnight excursions were made to Siena, for the Duccio *Maestá*; to Arezzo, for Piero de la Francesca; to Assisi for the Giottos; and to Ravenna for the mosaics. I was particularly fortunate in Arezzo, for just as I stepped out of San Francesco I spotted a bus labelled San Sepolcro, hopped on it, and after an hour's rather bumpy drive was rewarded by the wonderful 'Resurrection' in the Palazzo Publico – surely Piero's greatest painting. Ravenna was another eye-opener, for I had never before seen such superb mosaics as those in San Vitale and the Mausoleum of Galla Placidia.

At the end of this feast I returned to Hillie's villa for a few more days of luxurious living, before returning to London thoroughly refreshed in mind and body.

Then there was the holiday to Sicily with Myra and our American friend, Frank Mannheimer. At first we stayed at the Albergo Timeo in Taormina, where the orange-blossom was intoxicating, and the hotel, a delightful old family affair, was only a few steps from the Roman amphitheatre. The proprietor and his wife were extremely friendly. So much so that, just as we were leaving and Myra happened to mention the beautiful flower-arrangements in the hotel, the wife pressed into her unwilling arms one of the enormous brass dishes on which the flower-vases had rested. It was much too big to fit into the boot of our car, so Frank had to nurse it on the back seat.

Our first goal was Agrigento, where we duly admired the remains of the Greek temples. Then came the great surprise: for we hadn't known of Piazza Armerina, half way across the island, where the holiday-home of various Roman Emperors contains superb black-and-white floor mosaics, that can be viewed from cat-walks placed throughout the building. Moreover, it's all under cover.

Finally there was Palermo itself, where we wanted to go mainly to see the marvellous Norman mosaics in the Capella Palatina, so much finer than those in the larger and more famous Cathedral of Monreale, which we also visited. We had hoped to drive along the coast to Cefàlu to see the mosaic of *The Pantacrator* on the wall behind the altar, but unfortunately the skies opened and we decided not.

On our last day in Palermo, a Sunday, Frank steered us unerringly to what was obviously the best butcher in town. There I bought a large Salami Milano, as I always do when in Italy. When the butcher asked where it should be delivered on the following day, Frank explained in his best Italian that we wanted to take it with us, as we were leaving early in the morning. Alas, said the butcher, that was impossible: for although he was allowed to *sell* anything on a Sunday, the purchaser wasn't allowed to take it away. Brightly he asked, 'Have you a car?' When Frank said it was just outside, we were told to go and sit in it. Then there was a miniature procession from the shop with the butcher and his young assistant solemnly bearing the salami, which was duly presented to us in the car. Apparently this was perfectly all right, as we were not ourselves taking the object from the shop. As we sped off in triumph, Myra said, 'Trust Frank. He always gets what is wanted.'

In 1959, only six years before Myra's death, she and I were invited to a non-musical weekend in Paris by Sir Paul and Lady Mason. He was then our Ambassador to NATO, having previously been *en post* at The Hague, where Myra always stayed with them during her post-war tours in Holland. Among other entertainments, she and Lady Mason went to the races at Longchamps – Myra loved watching horses – while I went to a preview of the stained-glass windows commissioned from Chagall for the Medical Centre in Jerusalem. They were on display in a darkened annexe to the Louvre, where one could see them to perfection, with sunlight streaming in from outside. To round off our stay, Lady Mason drove us to Chartres for yet another visit to the glorious cathedral.

A later continental holiday combined prehistoric cave art with mediaeval stained glass. My companion was Tony Latham, who worked in the theatre department of the Victoria and Albert Museum. We started off from Hurn, near Bournemouth, on a plane that helpfully took my car as well as ourselves – it must have been one of the last of that convenient service. Then from Calais, through the growing warmth of the French countryside, to Les Eyzies, where we stayed at Les Glycines, a delightful auberge whose patron did the cooking (first-rate) while his wife kept the books. From there we visited the wonderful painted caves at Lascaux, luckily still open to the public. Then we went on to the stained-glass part of our tour: to Bourges, Poitiers and Anger, the last including the very early mediaeval tapestries in the Bishop's Palace. The churches at Moissac and Souillac were also visited, mainly for the wonderful sculpture in the former. Finally, to keep the best until the last, we stayed for a couple of nights in Chartres, so that Tony could have his first sight of the glass in the cathedral.

Most people find that conferences are more enjoyable for the personal contacts they provide than for the 'papers' they present. One of the first I went to was in Copenhagen, partly because it was not far from Lund, in Sweden, where I had to go in order to see a Schubert autograph. One day at lunch I found myself sitting beside a stranger. Out of the blue he said, 'I know who you are, but you don't know me!' It emerged that a mutual friend in London had told him to look out for me, and that he was Hugh Cobbe, later head of the music section of the British Library. Afterwards we went to a concert, which began with an enjoyable Nielsen symphony. When the next item started with a solo pianist stretching into the innards of the piano and plucking the strings with his fingers, I whispered to Hugh that I thought it was time for us to go and look for a meal in one of Copenhagen's excellent restaurants. Apart from my one-night visit to Lund, we spent the rest of the conference together, and have remained great friends ever since.

Occasionally we have made summer expeditions by car. On one of these we drove through France and Germany, where in Munich we enjoyed the pictures in the Alte Pinakotek and the beer, frankfurters and sauerkraut in the famous Hofbräuhaus. Our destination was a village in Austria called Alpbach, which lies at the end of a small road so has no through traffic. My niece Edith had been a skiing representative there for several seasons, so knew all the locals and was able to guide us to the nicest Gasthaus.

Another trip with Hugh was to visit two friends in France: Jacques de Froiard Brown and Kenneth Gilbert. I first met Jacques when he was a post-graduate student at Darwin College in Cambridge. He was studying agronomy, but I suspect was really interested in less earthy topics. Half-French and half-English, he wrote poetry in both languages and was passionately fond of music. On my return from a trip to America in 1969 I was astonished to learn that Jacques had become a monk at the Abbey of Solesmes in France. When Hugh and I visited him there we found the same Jacques as ever, ready to welcome us both with open arms. After he had shown us round the grounds, we went to the equivalent of Evensong, where I was pained to hear that the plainsong, for which Solesmes has long been famous, was accompanied by organ. I'm glad to say that at High Mass the following morning the men's voices were unaccompanied. After several years Jacques went back to Madagascar, where he had worked previously, to minister to the spiritual needs of the natives.

The Canadian, Kenneth Gilbert, I had met in London long before our French visit. A fine harpsichordist, he travels widely but lives in France. At the time of our visit his address was Le Chateau, Maintenon, *tout court*. This turned out to be less alarmingly grand than we feared, for the owners of the chateau had lent him the factor's house in the grounds, and there he lived with a friend who made harpsichords.

Another fortunate conference encounter was in London, when I got to know Dr Christopher R Wilson. He was already a Lecturer in Music at Reading University, but a year or so earlier had come to Cambridge to work on a post-graduate project. By an odd coincidence, he had occupied rooms in a Corpus house that was looked after by 'my' Phyllis, which immediately provided us with a connection. We soon became friends, and often met either at his house in Reading or mine in Cambridge. We too made motor trips in summer, either in England or abroad. One of these was again to visit Kenneth Gilbert, who by now had moved from Maintenon to a flat in Chartres. It had originally been part of the old Singing School, and was just opposite the North Portal of the cathedral. In the living-room there were three of his own harpsichords: the remaining three, as he told us airily, were in the local museum. As Chris had not been to Chartres before, I warned him how dark it was in the cathedral. What was our surprise when we discovered broad daylight inside. Apparently six of the stained-glass windows had been removed for repair; but as the rest were in their accustomed place, they could be properly admired. We were amused to find that whenever Kenneth went out in the morning to buy his daily baton of bread he always walked *through* the cathedral; but on his return journey, with baton in hand, he thought it more proper to walk outside the sacred edifice.

Another trip we made was to the west coast of Ireland, where I hadn't been since before the war. As one couldn't take one's car via Holyhead in those days, we flew to Dublin and there engaged a self-drive car. On our way to the west we stayed overnight in what had once been the Bishop's Palace in Cashel, but was now a delightful hotel. Nearby, on the Hill of Cashel, was what was left of the cathedral. Apparently one of the bishops had found the incline too steep for his carriage and horses, so had simply built himself a new cathedral in the town, and allowed the old one to become a ruin.

On we went to the magnificent Gap of Dunloe Hotel near Killarney. It is enormous, quite isolated, and looks as though it should be on a Swiss mountainside. Among the drives we took perhaps the finest was round the Ring of Kerry, where, in the little seaside village of Waterville, we happened on a pub called the Huntsman, which served the finest hot crab dish I have ever tasted. On first arriving in Dublin I had introduced Chris to genuine Guinness, which he had never tasted before. Thereafter we started every meal with a pint of the splendid beverage.

A much longer trip, part holiday and part work, took me for two months to America and Canada in 1969. It began in New York, with my usual visit to the El Greco *View of Toledo* in the Metropolitan Museum, plus two evening performances of Balanchine's New York City Ballet, which I had greatly admired on its solitary London season. The main attractions were Stravinsky's *Agon*, then comparatively new, and Ravel's *La Valse*; but other delights were included. After staying for a couple of nights with Myra's friends, Rose and Gene Parsonnet in New Jersey, I flew to the Grand Canyon, which Harold always said I must see before I die. Unfortunately he forgot that Flagstaff, where one stays, is rather high up, and that I don't like heights. When I got off the airport bus I strolled over to a low wall, took one look over, and saw the canyon yawning 1,000 feet below. Hurriedly I went into reverse and decided, after a severe nose-bleed, that one night in the hotel might suit me better than two. I must confess, however, that the colours of the canyon were remarkable, when viewed from the safety of my bedroom window.

On to San Francisco the next day, where I was met at the airport by Frank Mannheimer. We drove northwards over the Bay Bridge for about 25 miles to his house near Santa Rosa. It was built to his own design, and is perfectly situated in the middle of a wood on top of a small hill. It has every mod con, including a waste-disposal unit in the kitchen sink, which I soon made unusable by asking it to swallow artichoke leaves. Frank had to go off after only a few days, to take his annual summer class at Duluth on Lake Superior; but he had invited me to stay on for a month, while finishing the last volume of my *Early Keyboard Music* series. There was even an enormous Chevrolet in the garage, with power-brakes and -steering, which I had never encountered before. My first efforts at driving it were rather peculiar. But before long I managed to get the way of it, and even drove to Berkeley to see my friend Elizabeth Elkus. She is the widow of Albert, the former Head of Music at the university. He once told me that he and Ernst Bloch were great friends, though at one stage it appeared they were friends no longer. (Bloch was like that.) Then, when Albert was walking in Berkeley one day they bumped into one another round a corner; whereupon Bloch flung his arms around Albert and exclaimed, 'Let's forget all about it!' The only trouble being that Albert hadn't the faintest idea what it was they were to forget.

After my blissful stay in Frank's house, I flew on to Seattle, where Rann Hokanson (one of the quartet on our pre-war tour of Germany and Austria) lived with his wife Dorrie. Not only did they treat me royally, but they *drove* me, island-hopping all the way, to Victoria on Vancouver Island, which was my final port of call. I had been invited to talk at a piano teachers' conference, which was being held at the enormous Canadian Pacific Hotel – very comfortable and ever so slightly old-fashioned. It was the sort of place where people came for afternoon tea, and to listen to a trio of ladies playing sweet music. The walls of the immensely long passages were decorated with tinted photographs of European royalty, to whom one felt one ought to bow as one passed. But I should add that it was also the only hotel where I was asked, on phoning for breakfast in my room, whether I preferred my toast hot-buttered or cold; moreover, meals always arrived at the time they had been ordered.

The conference was made agreeable by the delightful President, Mrs Helen Dahlstrom, who, with her husband Alton, used to spirit me away for a quiet drink and to discuss the other lecturers. Later, whenever they came to London, they always visited me, and she still sends me a home-made Christmas pudding every year.

Another thing Harold told me I mustn't miss was the rail trip across the Rockies. How right he was! I caught the Canadian Pacific train at Vancouver – marvelling at the grass-grown end of the line that Pu's brother had helped to build – and in the luxurious comfort of a drawing-room car, woke up the next morning with towering mountains on either side. I only went as far as Edmonton, BC (I was told the rest of the rail journey is rather dull), where I stayed overnight and caught a plane to London the following morning. It had been a wonderful trip in every way, not least because I had been able to finish my edition of *Early English Keyboard Music* while at Frank's house.

Ever since before the war I had been interested in editing music. Generally it was for piano; but the first thing I tackled was an arrangement for string sextet or string orchestra of the marvellous six-part 'Fuga Ricercata' from Bach's *Musikalisches Opfer*, BWV 1079. Charles Rosen has since shown that it was almost certainly intended for solo keyboard; but when published during Bach's lifetime each 'voice' was printed on a separate stave to indicate its individuality, as in *Die Kunst der Fuge* (BWV 1018) and similar semi-didactic works. It was therefore generally assumed that more than a single instrument was required for performance. (It sounds magnificent on strings, so I must confess I don't regret having made the arrangement.)

When my partnership with Yfrah Neaman was established during the war, editing consisted mainly in 'realising' the keyboard part of compositions for violin and continuo. But there were other works that attracted me. The first I took on was Mozart's very early Sonata in C, K19d, for piano duet. It was probably written in London in 1765, for Mozart to perform with his sister at the Crown and Anchor tavern in the City, 'the keyboard being covered with a cloth', as the *Daily Advertiser* invitingly put it. Though certainly not great music, it is good to have yet another example of what that extraordinary boy was writing at the age of nine.

The next work to fascinate me was Bach's four-movement Suite in C minor (BWV 997), possibly for lute, whose only available source during the immediate post-war years was the unconvincing version for harpsichord in Volume 45 of the Bach-Gesellschaft edition. Bach's autograph has not survived, so the sources for this version were keyboard arrangements by various copyists. In them the right-hand part is almost invariably shown an octave higher in relation to the left-hand part than in any of Bach's genuine keyboard works. Moreover, the compass extends most improbably from the A flat below the bass stave to the high F above the treble.

It has been suggested that the suite, with the right hand of the Bach-Gesellschaft edition lowered an octave, was written specially for the celebrated lutenists Sylvius Leopold Weiss and Johann Kropfgans when they visited Bach at Leipzig in 1739. This is certainly possible. But I myself suspect that the suite was written for Lautenclavicymbal (lute-harpsichord), a rare instrument that combined the tone-quality of a lute with the keyboard of a single-manual harpsichord. Bach is known to have possessed two such instruments at the time of his death, and he was not the man to have instruments in the house without writing something for them.

I therefore felt justified in making a version of the suite for piano or harpsichord, in which the right-hand part of the Bach-Gesellschaft edition was as a general rule transposed an octave downwards. The only exceptions to this simple procedure lay in four very short passages (totalling half a dozen bars) in the second movement, the Fuga. Here, by referring to two copyists' different versions, it seemed reasonably possible to arrive at what Bach originally wrote.

In 1957 I decided to make more readily available the five fascinating pieces by William Tisdall from the *Fitzwilliam Virginal Book*. To these I added a 'Coranto' and a 'Jig' by 'Tisdale' from the *John Bull Virginal Book*, as they were the only other pieces that might have been by the same composer, though rather different in style. Nothing whatever is known about Tisdall; but probably he was a friend of the Tregian family of Cornwall, as his splendid *Pavana Chromatica* is sub-titled 'Mrs Katherine Tregian's Pavan'. The Tregians were a recusant family, of whom one, Francis the Younger, occupied his time in the Fleet Prison by writing out the *Fitzwilliam Virginal Book*.

I showed the manuscript of my edition of these seven pieces to Thurston Dart, who, in addition to being an outstanding musicologist and harpsichordist, was a director of the music-publishers Stainer & Bell. He said he would like his firm to publish it in their *Early Keyboard Music* series; which led to my showing Dart all my subsequent editions of early music, including the complete keyboard works of Purcell (as far as they were then known), the keyboard works of Croft and Dagincour, and the six Suites of John Blow.

Editing in earnest began after the war, when the Associated Board of the Royal Schools of Music invited me to edit the five books of graded piano pieces they published yearly for their examinations. I said I would be delighted to do so on two conditions: 1) that the work should always be done from photocopies of either the autograph or the original edition; and 2) that only genuine keyboard music should be used, ie, no arrangements. Curiously enough, these conditions had not always been observed in the past. My work on the grade-books continued for fifteen years, always with the helpful co-operation of two successive publication-managers, Frederick Freeman and Alan Jones.

At much the same time the Oxford University Press asked me to edit a series of anthologies, each volume of which was to be devoted to a single problem of keyboard technique. I felt that this idea was impractical, as far too many volumes would be required. Instead, I suggested to them four volumes, to be entitled *Style and Interpretation*, dealing respectively with 'Early Keyboard Music of France and England', 'Early Keyboard Music of Germany and Italy', 'Classical Piano Music', and 'Romantic Piano Music'. These proved to be so successful that they were followed-up by four pairs of volumes devoted to the *Early Keyboard Music* of respectively France, Germany, Italy and England. Eventually the introductions to each of these volumes were combined in a book entitled *Keyboard Interpretation*, and two volumes of 'Keyboard Duets' were added to the original series.

While still occupied with the final volumes of *Early Keyboard Music*, I happened to be staying in Glasgow with my late friend Jon Wight Henderson, then head of the piano department at the Scottish National Academy of Music. One evening he remarked what a pity it was that there was no good English edition of Schubert's Piano Sonatas: would I think of making one? I said it was something that had never occurred to me; but since I was very fond of Schubert I would think seriously of his suggestion. I did so, and asked The Associated Board whether they would be interested in an edition based on the autographs and first editions, also including the torsos of all the unfinished sonatas? Their reply was Yes. So the next two years were devoted to collecting the necessary source-material.

Most of this was obtained without difficulty, but there were exceptions: two involving public libraries and one a private collection.

The many Schubert autographs that belong to the Stadt- und Landesbibliotek in Vienna include almost all the unfinished sonatas, which of course I required. I wrote more than once to the head of the relevant department, but to no avail. He never bothered to reply, much less send me the microfilms. In despair, I sent a complaint to the Director of the Library. He must have stuck a pin in the official concerned, for in the end I did receive everything that was needed.

The autograph of the A minor Sonata (D 784) was left to the University of Lund, in Sweden, on condition that no photographs of it were supplied to anyone. I'm glad to say that this absurd prohibition has now been lifted – but not soon enough to save me from going all the way to Lund in order to look at the manuscript.

The difficulty with a private collection in Switzerland was much more serious, for it contained the autographs of the last three sonatas, the C minor (D 958), A major (D 959) and B flat major (D 960), without which the edition could not possibly be made. I sent the owner of the collection three requests for microfilms, two in English and (in case he didn't know that language) one in German. As all my letters remained unanswered I was at a loss to know what to do next. Then, by a lucky chance, I was visiting friends in France, just across the border from Basle. On hearing my tale of woe, one of them said, 'Leave it to me'. He looked up the collector's number in the phone book, got through to his wife (whom he described to me as 'the prize cow of all time'), and asked whether by any chance a letter from HF had arrived concerning the Schubert autographs? 'I have no idea', she replied, 'all letters concerning the collection go straight into the waste-paper basket.' After talking to her for half an hour, my persuasive friend managed to extract the following rigmarole from the lady. If HF would write to the Library of Congress in Washington, they would write to Basle for permission to copy the required items from the library's microfilms of the collection (made in case of war damage); permission would be granted from Basle; Washington would write to HF for the necessary payment; HF would send it; and finally the microfilms would be despatched. This entire process, from my first letter to Basle to the arrival of the films, took exactly two years. But it was worth it.

When the three large volumes of sonatas had been published, I suggested to The Associated Board that it seemed a pity not to publish Schubert's miscellaneous piano works also. Once again they agreed. Fortunately the source material of these was less difficult to obtain than that of the sonatas. Indeed, photographs of the autograph of the *Four Impromptus* (D 899) were given to me by the mother of its then owner, an American university professor who had loaned it to the Library of Princeton during his absence in Europe. (The autograph has since been acquired by the Pierpont Morgan Library in New York.) Moreover, the owners of the *'Wanderer' Fantasie* (D 760) sent me photographs of the autograph without even being asked.

Eventually the miscellaneous piano works were published in seven smaller volumes – the 400-odd dances were not included. When they were finished I couldn't resist adding an eighth volume devoted to two groups of waltzes that Myra Hess had included in her programmes. In all, the edition of Schubert's solo piano works had occupied me off and on for eleven years.

This did not end my work for The Associated Board. They issued a 15-volume *Anthology* of pieces chosen by Alan Jones from those I had already edited for the yearly grade books. Moreover, I edited for them over 40 volumes of varied works by Scarlatti, CPE Bach, Haydn, Mozart, Beethoven, Brahms and others, that either they required or I wanted to do.

The source material used in making The Associated Board editions – or rather, all of it that belonged to me – has been given to the Pendlebury Library in the Faculty of Music, the University of Cambridge, where it can be consulted by arrangement with the Librarian. It comprises some 250 items.

After my four-year burst of composition at the beginning of the 1950s there was a gap of two years, occupied mainly by playing and editing. Then, in fairly close succession, came my final two works, both on a large scale for vocal soloist, chorus and orchestra. The first was *Amore Langueo* (with solo tenor) to an anonymous English poem of the 14th century; and the second *The Dream of the Rood* (with solo soprano or tenor) to an English translation of an anonymous Anglo-Saxon poem. They arose in curiously different ways. *Amore Langueo* (completed in 1956) had haunted me ever since I first read the poem in *The Oxford Book of Verse* 25 years earlier. I had even made discontinuous sketches for parts of the music, but couldn't find the right beginning. When that eventually appeared in 1955 the work proceeded without a hitch. I even found to my astonishment that each isolated sketch fitted into its context without change of key. It was as though I was completing a jigsaw puzzle of which the pieces already existed.

The whole of this process, as I say, took twenty-five years. On the other hand, *The Dream of the Rood* (completed in 1958) had a stranger if less prolonged genesis. When recovering from 'flu a year earlier I happened to read Kingsley Amis's novel *Lucky Jim*, which at one point refers disparagingly to 'that awful Anglo-Saxon poem, "The Dream of the Rood"'. I had never even heard of it; but the moment I read that I knew I was going to set it. The only trouble was that I didn't know Anglo-Saxon; nor were any of the existing translations suitable. I was discussing the problem with my friends the Navarros, when Toty's wife Dorothy quietly asked, 'Would it be of any help if I were to make you a literal translation?' This was exactly what I wanted. She did so, and I immediately set it almost word for word.

Curiously enough since I am an unbeliever, both poems are specifically Christian. One of the two versions of *Amore Langueo* is Christ's complaint to his beloved, faithless Man; while *The Rood* represents the Cross on which Christ died. My friend Alan Ridout neatly explained the apparent anomaly when he wrote, 'It is an interesting paradox that some of the most powerful settings of religious texts have been the work of composers who were unbelievers or unconventional in belief... Imaginative commitment in an artist need not imply a commitment outside the imaginative act or object which is the result of it.' And there I rest my case.

The works were first conducted by Dr Herbert Sumsion (always known as 'John') at the Three Choirs Festivals in Gloucester, in respectively 1956 and 1959, when the soloists were Eric Greene and Heather Harper. The latter astonished me by singing through *The Rood* faultlessly when first shown the manuscript.

At the 1956 Festival Gerald Finzi had conducted the first performance of the full-orchestral version of his *In Terra Pax*. This is the work he had conceived so many years before at nearby Chosen Hill. It is peculiarly bitter, therefore, that it should have been there, on a motor trip with Vaughan Williams and his wife Ursula, that he caught chicken-pox. Normally this can be easily dealt with; but not if you have

Hodgkin's Disease, which Gerald had suffered from for five years. After only a short illness, he died at the Radcliffe Infirmary in Oxford on 27 September.

After completing *The Rood* I continued for more than a year to make sketches of various works – in particular for a string quartet that I had long wanted to write. But I found I was merely repeating myself, so decided it was time to stop composition. It was a hard decision to make, but made easier by the fact that there was still much editing to be done.

For some time I had been feeling that London, much as I loved it, was getting too dirty and noisy for me. Three burglaries and a series of unsatisfactory housekeepers following Betty's death (one of them an Austrian schizophrenic) hadn't helped. In about 1970 I told both Yfrah and Denis that I was going to stop playing in public (I wanted them to have plenty of time to look around for new partners); and in 1972 I definitely decided to move. The only question was, Where to? Ever since coming to London at the age of 14 I never thought of living anywhere else, so I had no preconceived ideas.

As if by magic, the problem was solved, at least for the moment. I received a totally unexpected invitation from Corpus Christi College in Cambridge to spend the Michaelmas term there as a Fellow Commoner. This invitation was generally reserved for school-masters needing a break from their usual work. But on this occasion it was decided – for the only time, I think – to give it to a musician. I suspect this was due to gentle pressure exercised by my friend Stuart Elliot, who was a Fellow, on the then Master of the College, Sir Duncan Wilson, a passionate lover of music. Be that as it may, I was delighted to accept the invitation, which gave me the perfect opportunity for continuing my Schubert editing free from interruptions and in delightful surroundings.

Interlude V: Arnold van Wyk (1916-1983)

Late in December 1941 I first got to know Arnold van Wyk – always known as Nols, the shortened form of Arnoldus, his Afrikaans name. He was still studying at the Royal Academy of Music, in his final year as a Performing Right Society scholar from South Africa; but he had already started part-time work as a translator and news-reader in the recently formed Afrikaans Section of the BBC, as he was unable to return to South Africa because of the war.

The head of the section, who knew Myra personally, wrote to her saying that a member of his staff was a composer: might it be possible to include some of his music in the National Gallery Concerts? As Myra's assistant, I was asked to look into the matter; and, being all too used to such offerings, my heart sank at the thought of having to write yet another letter saying we were afraid the music was not altogether suitable for the concerts. What was my astonishment when I received an elegantly-written manuscript – obviously the work of an accomplished composer – of Nols's *Five Elegies for String Quartet*. I was immensely impressed by their beauty and originality, so before long they were given their first public performance by the Menges String Quartet at the Gallery.

Thereafter we met frequently – sometimes at a Gallery concert, or when I went to the BBC Studios to hear one of the music programmes he had arranged. Often, too, he would stay with us at 106 Wildwood Road for several days at a time, in order to get some respite from the nightly bombings of central London, where he had a flat just off Baker Street. In the evenings we relaxed by making music. Generally it would be with one of the wonderful piano duets by Mozart or Schubert. But sometimes we moved to two pianos (the Bechstein upright was still in the studio) in order to explore the Mozart Piano Concertos, or the Bach Organ Trio Sonatas. (By modern standards the latter were scarcely 'authentic' performances, but it was a splendid way of getting to know the works.) We rarely allowed these sessions to be interrupted by air-raid warnings – which doubtless accounted for a rather peculiar neighbour reporting me to the police for 'signalling to enemy aircraft', because he so often heard the piano being played during air-raids!

Besides his *Five Elegies*, Nols had already written a Violin Concerto and his First Symphony while at the Academy, all of which were first performed there. The symphony was later conducted by Sir Henry Wood for a BBC broadcast on Union Day 1943, and by Sir John Barbirolli at the Cheltenham Festival. Works completed after we met, but while he was still in England, included the *Three Improvisations on Dutch Folk Songs* for piano duet, which Denis Matthews and I introduced at a Gallery Concert; and a longer duet work, *Poerpasledam* (Afrikaans for 'Pour passer le temps'), which Myra Hess and I played, also at the Gallery. (Much later this work was re-written for flute and piano.) More significant were the extensive sketches made for such works as the First String Quartet (alas, there was never to be a second), and the great song-cycle *Van Liefde en Verlatenheid* (*Of Love and Loneliness*) to poems by Eugène Marais. It was altogether typical that the first sketches for his unaccompanied *Missa in illo tempore* should have been jotted down in 1945, just 30 years before the work's completion.

Nols made many musical friends in England, among them Dennis Brain, the miraculous young horn-player who was so tragically killed in a motor-cycle accident; the pianist Noel Mewton Wood, to whose memory the *Night Music* is dedicated; and Jean Stewart, for whom the *Duo Concertante* for viola and piano was written. Another great friend was Ursula Vaughan Williams, both before and after her marriage to RVW, who, when Nols first knew her, lived at the unlikely address of 7½ Thayer Street. If an air-raid started while he was there, or he couldn't face the dark walk home through Marylebone Cemetery, he would be tucked up on a sofa for the night.

When the easing of wartime travel restrictions enabled Nols to return to South Africa in December 1946, after an absence of eight years, his friends in England missed him sorely. Fortunately, however, it was au revoir rather than goodbye, for he came back to England on a number of working holidays, sometimes for a year or more. In return, I myself went to South Africa five or six times, at first combining my visits with concert tours, and later (when I had stopped playing in public) going for the sheer pleasure of being with Nols.

While I still lived in London he always stayed with us in Wildwood Road, where the Bechstein upright was moved to the spare room for his use. Then, after I moved to Cambridge, he happily made 51 Barton Road his English home. During several of his visits we made holiday trips: one to the Edinburgh Festival, where my Octet was being played; another to Vienna, Greece and Crete; and finally to a small house belonging to our friends Dirk la Cock and Dieter Bertram on the Greek island of Santorini.

My final visit to South Africa was after Nols had died on 27 May 1983. I stayed for three months at his house in Thibault Street, Stellenbosch, partly in order to help found the Arnold van Wyk Trust, whose main aim is to publish those of his works that have not yet appeared in print; and partly to tidy up the manuscripts themselves. Most of the latter could be dealt with on the spot; but two had to be brought back to England, as they would involve a good deal of time: 1) the making of a vocal score and English translation of the early *Kerskantate (Christmas Cantata)* for soloists, chorus and orchestra, originally commissioned by the South African Broadcasting Company; and 2) the disentangling of the *Duo Concertante* for viola and piano. Though the *Duo* had already been performed, the surviving autographs were a maze of emendations and alterations. Fortunately Nols had made these in several different coloured inks; and since he had always used the inks in a consistent sequence, it was possible to tell, without any doubt, which version was the latest. This I took to be what Nols intended as definitive.

The work has since been recorded on Claremont CD GSE 1525 by Gina Benkes and Melanie Horne, together with the *Five Elegies* and the String Quartet. The lovely orchestral *Primavera* and Symphonies I and II are available on Claremont CD GSE 1509, played by the Cape Town Symphony Orchestra conducted by Omri Hadari; and the *Night Music*, played by Jill Richards, on a composite record of South African Piano Music, Claremont CD GSE 1522.

Chapter Six: Corpus Christi College 1972

The 1st October 1972 was a gloriously sunny day for the drive from Wildwood Road to my temporary abode in Cambridge. I first of all called at Leckhampton House, the post-graduate section of Corpus, where Stuart Elliot was then the Warden. He guided me to Corpus itself, where we unloaded my goods and chattels at the pleasant set of rooms – a sitting-room and bedroom – that had been allotted to me. In many ways they were ideal. But the neighbouring church, St Benet's, did have bell-ringing practice every Friday evening; and the rooms of Michael Tanner, a charming philosophy don, were within easy earshot. As well as being a philosophy don he was an ardent Wagnerite; and *Der Ring des Nibelungen* was apt to start at 9am on Sunday mornings and continue relentlessly until the final D flat chords were heard around 6pm. But these were small considerations compared with the delights of being in Cambridge, with wonderful buildings to look at whenever you went shopping. By way of work, my Schubert edition had still to be completed; and for this the various libraries were invaluable. I mainly used the University Library, the Pendlebury Library in the Faculty of Music, and the Library of King's College, for although they possessed no Schubert autographs they often had early editions.

Generally I prepared breakfast and lunch in my own rooms. But for dinner I would don the gold-bordered gown of a Fellow Commoner and go into Hall. The conversation there was usually, but not invariably, easy. On one occasion I remarked to the man sitting opposite that I had known a previous occupant of his post. To this his only reply was a rather dry 'Oh'. Very different was Bruce Dickens, the Professor of Anglo-Saxon, with whom I gossiped about old churches. Once Stuart asked him whether he knew Henryson's poem *The Testament of Cresside* about which I had been enthusing? Bruce replied, 'If you have another look at the title-page you'll find that I was the editor.'

The Master of Corpus was then Sir Duncan Wilson, formerly our Ambassador in Moscow. He loved music, and used to come round to my house when his wife was away, for dinner and piano duets. Being really musical, he was always in the right bar even if the notes he played weren't always quite right. He had many friends among the musicians of Moscow, so it was no surprise that Rostropovitch came to the Master's Lodge when he first left Russia.

As 106 Wildwood Road would be empty while I was in Cambridge, I arranged for it to be redecorated during my absence. One morning I was having breakfast in my rooms when the phone rang. It was the foreman of the firm that was doing the redecorations, and he broke it to me that there had been a fire at my house! I asked whether I should come up immediately to inspect the damage. 'No', he said, 'wait until tomorrow when we'll have cleared up some of the mess.' (It was that sort of firm.) Apparently the workmen had arrived early in the morning to find clouds of smoke billowing through the front-door letter-box. On getting inside, they found that there was no staircase. An electrical fault had set the stairs alight; but mercifully the fire had not spread, because all the doors in the house had been left shut. The only serious casualties were the staircase and the poor little upright Bechstein. Years before, the piano had been moved to the spare-room, for Arnold's use during his visits; and as the spare-room was at the head of the staircase, the smoke and heat had done their worst on the piano. The Steinway was more fortunate. It was in the studio, with three intervening doors between it and the fire. Moreover, I had had the forethought to cover it with an old sheet. In spite of this, the legs were badly scorched. (More of this later.)

The thoughtful foreman had already had all the curtains taken down and the carpets taken up, and the lot sent to the cleaners; so there was little I could do other than return to Cambridge, having asked the firm to begin the redecorations all over again, and got in touch with my insurance company. By some miracle, none of the music or books in the house had been damaged.

Corpus was wonderfully helpful over the fire, and not only offered to house me for another term, but gave me the use of one of their post-graduate flats. In mid-December 1972, I therefore moved into 19c Cranmer Road, and remained there until the end of March 1973. The flat backed onto the grounds of Leckhampton, where I was given dining-rights, and was looked after by Mrs Phyllis Creek, one of the regular Corpus 'bedders'. When I told Phyllis I was thinking of coming to live in Cambridge permanently, and asked whether, if I found a suitable place, she would be able to look after it, she astonished me by saying, 'I would *love* to!' But alas, no suitable place was found while I was still in Cambridge.

As my work on Schubert had been completed, I looked around for something else to do. It was then that I realised there was no edition of *Anne Cromwell's Virginal Book* of 1638, that Anne had been a niece of Oliver, and that the Oliver Cromwell Museum in nearby Huntingdon was rumoured to possess the autograph. When I wrote asking for photographs of it, they replied that the manuscript really belonged to the London Museum, though it had been lent to them years ago and then conveniently forgotten. I therefore arranged for it to be photographed and got on with the editing, trusting that meanwhile the manuscript would be returned to the London Museum. The music it contains is not very important, but is of considerable interest on two counts: first, it helps to bridge the 50-year gap that separates *Parthenia or the Maydenhead of the first Musicke that ever was printed for the Virginalls* (1612/13) from its belated successor, *Musicks Hand-Maid* (1663); and second, it provides a revealing glimpse of the kind of keyboard music – mainly dances and arrangements of masque music – that was being played in the home during the second quarter of the 17th century.

Another shock awaited me some weeks after the fire at Wildwood Road. Steinways had already removed the piano to their warehouse to have the legs repolished. Again the phone rang one morning. It was Steinways to say that unfortunately there had been a fire in their warehouse the night before! I asked nervously how my piano had fared? 'Oh, it's quite all right', they replied, 'we turned it on its side and drained the water out.' They also said that of course they would give the piano a complete overhaul without charge. And when eventually it was returned to Wildwood Road, I must say it really was 'as good as new'. But two fires within as many weeks *did* seem a little hard.

By the end of March I was able to return to a rejuvenated 106 Wildwood Road after six most enjoyable months in Cambridge, and, to my great surprise and delight, having been made an Honorary Member of Corpus Christi College.

I had been back for only three months when Messrs Hockey and Sons, house-agents in Cambridge, phoned to say that 51 Barton Road had come on the market: would I care to come and have a look at it? I leaped into the car, drove up to Cambridge and stopped outside No 51. It looked most attractive; but alas was beside a main road and was probably too noisy for the comfort of a musician. However, I thought I might as well have a look at it, having come so far. As soon as I saw the inside of the downstairs living-room, I knew that the house was *not* too near the road, for I could install double-windows wherever necessary.

51 Barton Road is what looks like a two-storied 'addition' to a large three-storied house of about 1802; the whole place was originally advertised in the press as 'The house in the fields, with commodious outbuildings and a bowling-green'. It must indeed have been 'in the fields', for it is a mile from the Market Place, and would then have been on the very outskirts of Cambridge. Some years before I saw it, it had been cleverly transformed, turning the main house into four flats (two large and two small), leaving the two-storied 'addition' untouched, and building two terraces of smaller houses where the 'commodious outbuildings and bowling-green' once had been. There was still plenty of space between the main house and the new terraces for a charming garden, so the whole place well deserved the prize it received for an imaginative development.

Much of the charm of the living-room that so attracted me lay in the fact that it was on two levels. The higher part, at the far end, in fact formed the roof of a cellar that contained the central-heating boiler and space for odd junk; while the lower end had been used by the previous owners as a dining-room. Adjoining the living-room was a kitchen, perfectly new; and, on the floor above, a bathroom, also new, and three bedrooms, one fairly large and two medium-sized.

It seemed the perfect house for me; so, after the usual haggling, I bought the 96-year lease and moved in, with the help of my dear sister Sally, on 3 October 1973. It was one of the best things I ever did.

The Steinway and my writing-desk fitted comfortably into the lower half of the living-room, while the upper half served as a sitting-room. (I suspect the two halves were originally two separate rooms, for a central pillar now supported the floor above.) Upstairs the large bedroom was mine, while the other two were respectively a guest-room and the room containing the main part of my library of music and books on music. Bound volumes of music and art books remained on the shelves that had originally been made for them, which now, with a little extra carpentry, fitted neatly into the entrance-hall.

In due course the invaluable Phyllis came in for a couple of hours on two mornings a week, kept the house and its contents shining, and remained with me until she was taken seriously ill twenty-three years later.

Once I had settled into No 51 work continued much as before. When asked whether I would care to do some teaching, I declined; but became a member of the Music Faculty when told it would only entail an annual general meeting and a glass of Madeira.

Chapter Seven: 51 Barton Road, Cambridge 1973–

Before coming to live in Cambridge I often went to the fascinating concerts given in London by the Early Music Consort. Their founder and director, David Munrow, appeared to be able to play any instrument that was put in his hands; but he was, of course, surrounded by other expert string and wind players and also vocalists. One of the players I got to know well was Christopher Hogwood the harpsichordist, who could also be seen on occasion plucking the strings of a medieval harp. When Chris was a pupil of Thurston Dart in Cambridge, he was one of several young musicians who lodged in the house of the harpsichordist, Mary Potts. On one of my trips to Cambridge in search of early keyboard material, Chris introduced me to Mary; and when eventually I came to live there, she in turn introduced me to Lucy Boston.

Lucy was an extraordinary person. She lived at Hemingford Grey in a house that was said to date from the 11th century, and although herself 80 years old she was still an ardent gardener, who specialised in specie roses. At the age of 60 she had suddenly discovered she had a flair for writing children's books, and thereafter produced the 'Green Knowe' series, all based in one way or another on her own house. Though nominally 'children's books' I suspect that, like *Alice in Wonderland*, they are appreciated quite as much by grown-ups – certainly I've read all six of them more than once.

As Lucy was a passionate lover of music – particularly early music – she often gave small parties in her candle-lit upstairs music-room for half a dozen friends. If one of them admired the immense brick fireplace, she would say dismissively, 'Oh, it's only Elizabethan', then point out the much more interesting mediaeval entrance to the house, originally reached by an outside stone staircase. Music could be anything from a group of madrigals led by Emma Kirkby to instrumental works generally including the lutenist Anthony Rooley. The only thing you couldn't expect was any keyboard instrument larger than a clavichord or a spinet, for the simple reason that a harpsichord couldn't be negotiated up the narrow staircase. Afterwards we would repair to the downstairs living-room, where there was a real mediaeval stone fireplace, to enjoy chat and the food and wine provided by Lucy.

In 1978 a large group of my friends celebrated my 70th birthday with a splendid party in the concert hall of the Guildhall School of Music. Besides delicious refreshments, we were regaled with a programme of music consisting of piano duets played by Denis Matthews and his wife Brenda, my Second Violin Sonata by Yfrah Neaman and Denis, and the Schubert B flat Sonata by Stephen Kovacevich.

In my edition of the latter work I query one note in the slow movement, which in Schubert's autograph and almost all editions appears as an F in the context of three sharps (ie, F sharp). I feel sure it should be an F double-sharp, and that Schubert simply forgot the accidental (as he very often did) because it was so obvious. The passage appears twice in the movement. The first time round, Steve played an F sharp; but when the passage reappeared, with a demure glance at me, he played an F double-sharp. It was a charming gesture, which no one but myself would have noticed.

My friends also gave me a beautiful facsimile of Schubert's *'Unfinished' Symphony*, while the Finzi Trust gave me the very fine portrait of myself by Benedict Rubbra, son of the composer Edmund. Altogether it was a most moving occasion.

For some years I had been bothered by a small lump at the base of my right-hand little finger. An American surgeon friend told me it was the beginning of a Dupitron's Contraction, but I needn't worry about it, as it could easily be removed by a small operation. Eventually I had the operation done by a London surgeon recommended by my American friend. He said it would be a perfectly easy matter; but omitted to say that the operation *could* go wrong. Unfortunately in my case it *did* go wrong; with the result that ever since then I've been unable to stretch the chord of C major with my right hand. Not unnaturally, this has taken all the fun out of piano-playing, so my beloved Steinway sits in the corner, reproachful and unused. (It has since been given to Hugh Cobbe.)

Several years after Gerald Finzi's untimely death in 1953, Joy Finzi had moved to a delightful cottage, Bushey Leaze, in the Downs to the north of Newbury. As Hugh Cobbe and his wife Kate had established themselves in a village just south of Newbury, and Chris Wilson, now married to Christine, was already Warden of a students' residence at Reading University, I usually visited all three establishments whenever I drove down from Cambridge. On returning from one of these trips I began to feel rather odd. My sister Sally had had a similar attack in Ireland a year earlier; and as she had described her symptoms to me, I knew I was in for a coronary thrombosis. After being examined by the doctor, I was borne off in an ambulance to Addenbrooke's Hospital, where they looked after me splendidly in intensive care, and allowed me to go home after nine or ten days. Though still slightly wobbly, I was only too glad the attack hadn't occurred during the 80-mile drive from the south.

Stuart Elliot had been a great support to me while I was at Corpus. Not only did he accompany me to Hall, but we often went to concerts together or to the Arts Theatre (I had been an avid play-goer in London). He frequently came to Barton Road for dinner; or, for a change, we would go to the Graduate Centre or a local pub for a meal. Our favourite haunt was the Churchill, near Churchill College. Indeed it was there that something shocking occurred. At the end of a meal, without the slightest warning, Stuart suddenly collapsed over the dinner-table. An ambulance was phoned for; and as soon as it arrived, everything possible was done to resuscitate Stuart. But when I asked the ambulance-men whether I should follow them in my car to the hospital, they said they were afraid it would be no use, as they were going straight to the mortuary. It was a grievous blow, for we had been such good friends ever since we re-encountered one another in New York in 1953.

When my 80th birthday came round, Hugh Cobbe asked might he organise something similar to the Guildhall party ten years earlier. I said I would really prefer something a little more private this time. But there was no escape. Hugh gave a large dinner-party for me at Brooks's Club on the day itself; and other friends kept the ball rolling by further gatherings in their own homes. Moreover, the Birmingham BBC gave over one of their Friday Concerts to the celebration, including my own Octet and the Mozart Serenade for 13 Wind Instruments (of which I have been particularly fond ever since National Gallery days), and ending with a splendid party for all concerned.

In the following year I made a lightning trip to Edinburgh by air. It seemed rather a mad undertaking – particularly for a single night; but there had been a loan exhibition of paintings from all over the world at the recent Festival, and it included my beloved El Greco *View of Toledo* from New York. And as Edinburgh is considerably closer than America, I decided I must go. Three years earlier I had been to Madrid and Toledo to see the El Grecos there, so it seemed only right to round off the experience with what I have always felt to be his greatest painting. Incidentally, one of the most exciting surprises at the Prado in Madrid were the Goyas: for I had never before realised what a great painter he was, nor how varied was his range.

Between 1984 and 1995 most of my compositions were recorded on CDs. The first two to appear were subsidised by the Finzi Trust and the remaining three by the RVW Trust. It was a great satisfaction to have such fine performances on record, to join the 78s made by Myra Hess and the Griller Quartet during the war. Just recently I have had the delightful surprise of receiving through the post – I don't know from whom – the excellent Biddulph re-issue of Myra's 1938-42 HMV recordings, including Schumann's *Carnaval*, my own Sonata, and what she used to call 'a greep of pouces'.

Of special interest to me were also the CDs of the Hungarian pianist András Schiff. Richard Butt had heard him play Bach's *'Goldberg' Variations* at the Birmingham BBC, and was so impressed that he engaged him to play the same work at a special concert at one of the Aldeburgh Festivals. He told me I must be there, and indeed it was most impressive: the only Bach playing I have ever heard that reminded me in its clarity and warmth of Harold's. Later, András made a CD of all the Bach *'English' Suites*, and another of a selection of Scarlatti sonatas, for both of which he asked me to write the accompanying booklets.

As my editing for the Associated Board had by then been completed, I looked around for other things to do. Having always enjoyed entertaining friends to a meal, I had collected a vast number of recipes over the years – always recipes that did not require the cook to abandon his guests, while disappearing into the kitchen for last-minute preparations. As I didn't know of any cookbook written from precisely that point of view, I put all the recipes in order, added some collecting links, typed them out, and my friend Chris Wilson named the result

Entertaining Solo. The book was intended primarily as a gift to my friends and to the Finzi Trust (who had subsidised my first two CDs); so I had it designed by another friend – the professional book-designer Jeremy Greenwood – and had it privately printed. (I was rather proud of the spiral-binding, my own idea, which allows the book to stay open at the required page.) The astonishing thing is that a Japanese friend of mine, Nosomu Hayashi, who was then helping to catalogue the Japanese holdings in the University Library, said one day, 'Would you allow me to translate the book into Japanese?' I was only too delighted; since when it has been published in instalments in a monthly magazine in Tokyo, and is now appearing there in book form.

Next I decided to write a small book on piano duets – ie, two players on *one* piano. Partly because they were what Denis Matthews and I had played together for 25 years; but also because the repertoire is very fine and too little known. The Oxford University Press, who were interested in the idea, asked that two-piano music should be included; so I followed their suggestion, and the result appeared in 1995 under the title *Keyboard Duets*.

Now, on the assumption that it's always wise to have something on hand, I've embarked on this memoir.

One of the great pleasures of being in Cambridge was to get to know Reiner Schneider-Waterberg. We were introduced at the West Road Concert Hall, Cambridge, in November 1992, when, much to my surprise, he said he'd been wanting to meet me for some time. When I asked Why?, he replied that we had mutual friends in Stellenbosch, South Africa, where he had been to University. Born in 1967 in Namibia, formerly German South West Africa, he knew several people to whom Arnold had introduced me. He was now at St John's College, Cambridge, on a South African scholarship, supposedly working for a PhD on International Relations, but quite obviously more interested in being a countertenor in the chapel choir at Trinity.

When he first came to Barton Road he asked whether I had written anything for countertenor, to which I replied, 'Alas, no'. Then a couple of days later I remembered that I *had* once written a song for countertenor and harp, for inclusion in Alastair Sim's 1958 London production of William Golding's play *The Brass Butterfly*. I didn't even have a copy of it, so wrote to the Bodleian Library in Oxford (which has all my autographs), asking them to send me photostats of the sketches for the song. When they arrived I managed to piece them together and make a new version for countertenor and *piano*; which explains how the song *Love and Reason* came to be published as recently as 1993, and why it is dedicated to Reiner.

Since then we have met often, both at Barton Road and in Trinity Chapel, where I specially remember his singing the alto solos in Gibbons' *This is the Record of John*, and in Bach's *St John Passion*.

In 1993 I had determined to go to Chartres while still mobile, to see yet again the glass in the cathedral – a fifth visit, my first having been with Harold in pre-war days. As Reiner had never been there, I invited him to come too. While we were strolling by the river in the old part of the town, he told me of a plan he had concocted for giving a concert at West Road to celebrate my 85th birthday. In fact, because of earlier engagements, the concert was given in the following February. But on Trafalgar Day 1993 I gave a small dinner-party at the Garden House Hotel for Kathleen Lee (widow of a former Master of Corpus), Anne McBurney, my niece Edith, and Reiner himself.

When he disappeared half way through dinner, I assumed he had gone to the loo; but not at all. Suddenly the door to our private room was flung open and in marched Reiner with seven of his fellow Trin-Men (members of the Chapel Choir) lustily singing *Happy Birthday to You*. They then entertained us to half an hour of unaccompanied vocal music, ranging from William Byrd to George Gershwin. It was one of the nicest surprises I have ever had.

The celebratory concert, 'Howard Ferguson and Friends', duly took place at West Road on 26 February 1994, and included three of Vaughan Williams' *Blake Songs*, Arnold van Wyk's *Vier Weemoedige Liedjes*, Gerald Finzi's clarinet *Bagatelles*, and five of my own pieces. The performers (all students) were Richard Ormrod (piano), Tim Horton (piano), Mark Adami (oboe d'amore), Stuart Stratford (clarinet), Reiner Schneider-Waterberg (countertenor), and Nell Catchpol (violin). Afterwards the participants, their friends and my friends all repaired to the Garden House Hotel for more substantial celebrations. When I asked one of the performers how they managed to fit in all the practice required, he answered, 'Quite easy: we just don't do the work we should be doing!'

In the late spring Reiner and I went for a marvellous ten days to the Schubertiade in Feldkirch, Austria, staying in a delightful flat 1000 feet up on the Viktorsberg, five or six miles away. A self-drive car from Zürich Airport enabled us to go wherever we liked, which included an overnight excursion to Innsbruck, to visit the choir from Bad Tölz with which Reiner had visited Russia earlier in the year.

On our return to England we made two further excursions: one, to see Stravinsky's *The Rake's Progress* at the new Opera House at Glyndebourne; and the other to Swindon (of all places), where Richard Butt was conducting a friend's choir in *Messiah*, and had invited Reiner to be alto soloist.

At the end of the academic year of 1994 Reiner left Cambridge, to continue his vocal studies at the Mozarteum in Salzburg and later at the Schola Cantorum Balisiensis. But he came back to Cambridge now and again; and in the spring of 1995 we made a splendid tour in Germany, to see as many of Riemenschneider's sculptures as possible, a treat I had long promised myself.

It's strange that the age-difference of almost 60 years should have made so little difference to our friendship. But how fortunate for me.

Postlude: Music Autographs and Sources

Though I've always been fascinated by composers' autographs and first editions, I've never had any desire to collect them. Nevertheless, a number have come my way, either fortuitously or in connection with my editing work. By way of 'postlude', and for the record, I should recount the circumstances of how I came to possess them, and where they are now to be found. They are listed here in the order in which I encountered them.

Elgar

My only meeting with Elgar was on 30 October 1928, when he came to lunch at the country home of his old friend Edward Speyer, a great music-lover and collector of both musicians and their autographs. (Harold, Ivor James and I had been invited for the weekend.) It was just six years before Elgar's death, at the sad time of his life when he felt his works were no longer appreciated and claimed he was more interested in horse-racing than in music. Nevertheless, he displayed considerable curiosity when he saw the contents of a manilla folder that Speyer handed to him. 'Goodness', he exclaimed, 'I'd forgotten all about that.'

It was an autograph full score of the 'Dream Interlude' ('Jack Falstaff... page to Thomas Mobray, Duke of Norfolk') from his own Symphonic Study *Falstaff*, complete and self-contained, but in G minor instead of its definitive key of A minor. It must have been written and scored before the rest of the work, then transposed in order to fit into its final context.

The autograph now belongs to an English private collection, and should not be confused with the group of piano-score sketches for the same interlude (also in G minor) on folios 3-6 of Add MS 63161 in the British Library.

Mozart

Harold and I used to stay at the old Lion Hotel in Petty Cury when we visited Toty de Navarro in Cambridge. After breakfast one morning he was sitting talking to us when in walked a gentleman in a rather scruffy-looking raincoat, carrying a brown-paper parcel under his arm. He was introduced as Mr Ralph Griffin. When he heard Harold's name he immediately said, 'Oh, I think you might be interested in this.' The parcel was then opened, to reveal the autographs of Mozart's two late Sonatas for Piano Duet, the F major, K 497, and the C major, K 521. Pointing to the first page of the F major, he said, 'Look where the careless fellow has spilled his coffee!' In those happy days before prices became astronomical, Griffin was in the habit of going to auctions and bidding for music autographs that looked interesting. He was now on his way to present the wonderful pair to the Fitzwilliam Museum, where they remain to this day.

Schubert

As already indicated, all the photographs and microfilms of autographs and first editions used in the Associated Board edition of Schubert's piano works have been given to the Pendlebury Library, Faculty of Music, the University of Cambridge, where they can be consulted by arrangement with the Librarian.

Stanford

When Harold Samuel died in 1937 he left me his books and music. Among several works by Stanford were three autographs and two first editions. The autographs included two unpublished fugues for piano: *Fuga à 3*, dated December 1922, and *Fuga à 4*, dated January 1923; the first inscribed 'A Christmas Card for Sammy for many kindnesses, CVS', and the second, 'Here is a New Year's Card! Please tell me if it arrives safely! for HS. I hope I have put in all the beastly accidentals. Probably not. CVS.' The third autograph was of an unpublished *Ballata & Ballabile*, Op 160, for solo cello and piano (in fact orchestra), dated 29 May 1918. Stanford had asked HS to show it to the Portuguese cellist, Guilherminia Suggia, in the hope that she would play it. She didn't, and the MS remained in Harold's library.

The first editions were of two of the books of the first set of *48 Preludes in all the Keys* (1919), Op 163, inscribed and dedicated to HS, who had given their first performance.

The five works now belong to the British Library.

Parry and Walton

These four autographs were given to me by my old friend Dr Emily Daymond, to whom I fear they did not rightly belong. Dayme, as we called her, was a remarkable woman. She was one of the original students at the Royal College of Music when it opened in 1883, and later, as the first woman Doctor of Music in England, she was put in charge of music at the newly opened Royal Holloway College for Women at Egham in Surrey. When I got to know her in the mid-1920s she was presiding over the Parry Room Library at the RCM. She was brisk in manner and movement, deep-voiced, voluble, and boundlessly kind to the teenager who kept bothering her with requests for volumes of the Bach-Gesellschaft. It soon became clear that she had been devoted to Parry, for whom she acted as a kind of unpaid musical secretary – Gerald Finzi used to say that she wrote his semiquavers for him – and whenever we met the conversation invariably veered towards Parry and his music. She would then go to a large tallboy in the corner of her sitting-room, scrabble like a terrier in one of its drawers, and triumphantly produce the autograph of the very work we had been discussing. (Much later I learnt that these had been borrowed from Parry himself over the years, but never returned.)

On one occasion she brought out the autographs of two of Parry's unpublished piano pieces, Nos 2 and 5 of the *Five Miniatures* which she herself edited for Curwen in 1926. After we had looked at them for a few minutes she suddenly said in her decisive way, 'You must have them, dear.' Rather startled, I replied that it was terribly kind of her but I couldn't possibly take them. 'Nonsense,' she said, 'I'd love you to have them.' In the end, realising that they would be safer in my keeping than in hers, I took them home and put them away carefully in a folder. After Dayme died, I gave them to the Bodleian Library in Oxford, where most of Parry's autographs are housed.

Several years later, to my even greater astonishment, she produced from the same tallboy two rather scruffy-looking little manuscripts, each containing a few sheets of 12-stave music-paper torn in half and covered with clear but childish writing. One contained an organ chorale prelude in six flats (very daring!) dated 16 August 1916; the other a setting of Shakespeare's *Tell me where is fancy bred?* for three voices, three violins and piano, dated 2 July 1916. 'Whatever are these?', I asked. 'Well', she replied, 'it was like this. About twenty years ago I was sitting next to Henry Ley at lunch at the College – you know, dear, he was organist at Christ Church, Oxford. Well, he told me they had a perfectly extraordinary 14-year-old boy in the choir who did nothing but write music; he then asked would I like to see some of it? I said Yes! So he took these two little pieces out of his briefcase and passed them to me; I took them home, and I'm afraid they've been here ever since. They're by Willie Walton, so I'm sure you'd like to have them.' After the usual protests, and for the same reason as before, I took them home and put them in a safe place. The sequel was even more bizarre.

After Dayme's death I found that the British Museum (now the British Library) would be only too glad to have them, as Walton's publisher (the Oxford University Press) had kept virtually all his other autographs. Thus they came to be entered in the Library's catalogue as Add MS 52384.

Some years later I had an agitated phone call from the Oxford University Press: What were these two pieces by Walton that I had given to the Library and about which he knew nothing? I explained how they had been acquired and guaranteed their authenticity. The information was passed on to Walton, who was doubtless not best pleased to learn of the survival of these childhood efforts. Nevertheless, they are now listed as items 2 & 3 in Stewart Craggs'

William Walton: a Thematic Catalogue; Oxford University Press, London 1977. (Item No 1 is the much more accomplished *A Litany* for unaccompanied voices, dated Easter 1916, which Walton revised for publication by the OUP in 1930.)

Butterworth

On the death of R O Morris in 1948 I was surprised to find not only that he had bequeathed me the royalties in all his books, but also that I was his sole executor. The latter provision caused considerable consternation, as I was just about to leave for a four-month visit to South Africa. However, his estate was eventually settled up without too much difficulty.

It contained very little music, of which the only two items I acquired were a miniature score of Stravinsky's *Histoire du Soldat* (lent to R O by myself many years earlier), and a manuscript full score of Butterworth's *On the Banks of Green Willow*, a work of which I was and am particularly fond. I was quite sure that the manuscript was in R O's writing; and as he had been a great friend of Butterworth – who was killed in World War I – it was quite likely that he would have copied a score for himself before the work was published. Not until some years later did I begin to wonder: was the manuscript really written by R O? To solve the problem I went first to the Library of the English Folk Song and Dance Society near Regent's Park, which owns Butterworth's folksong notebooks; then to the Bodleian Library in Oxford, to which his other autographs belong. On comparing their holdings with my score of *The Banks of Green Willow* it became perfectly clear that the latter was not in R O's writing at all, but in Butterworth's. I had simply been misled by the unusual similarity between the two men's manuscript. Moreover, the Bodleian already possessed the autograph from which the work had been engraved; and as mine was different in several respects, and obviously earlier, the Library was delighted to add it to its collection.

Gurney

The full story of Ivor Gurney's autographs is told in Michael Hurd's admirable biography, *The Ordeal of Ivor Gurney* (Oxford University Press, 1978). Suffice it to say that they came temporarily into Gerald Finzi's hands in the mid-1930s, when Gurney was already in an asylum following the 1914 war. They consisted mainly of a large number of songs and many hundreds of poems.

As the autographs had not even been catalogued, our first aim was to go through all the songs (the accompaniments played by myself, while Gerald supplied the voice part in the upper reaches of the piano), list them (Joy

Finzi's task), and classify them roughly into three categories: 1) should be published; 2) could be published; and 3) unpublishable. From category 1) we chose what we felt to be the 30 best songs; took them to Vaughan Williams and played them to him; he then made the final choice of 20 songs, which were duly published in two volumes by the Oxford University Press in 1938. Since then, other volumes have appeared; while most of the poems, painstakingly typed out by Joy Finzi, have also been published.

The autographs are now in the Gloucester Public Library.

Grieg and Bax

When I was dealing with Myra Hess's music after her death in 1965, I encountered a curious problem. There was a printed volume of Grieg's songs, the *Albumblätter*, Op 2, which she had never mentioned to me, though it was unusual in several respects. For one thing, the music text contained a number of ink corrections; and for another, there was an ink inscription (unsigned) on the cover 'to M.P.', the initials of Frau Minna Peterson, the dedicatee of the songs. These facts suggested that it could well be a first edition with corrections in the composer's hand. When I sent it to the Grieg Museum in Bergen they confirmed that this was indeed so; moreover, they were delighted to add the copy to their library, not only because of tbe autograph corrections, but because they did not already possess the first edition. In return they kindly sent me a catalogue of their library.

Another work posed no problems, though again I had not known it was there. It was an autograph of Arnold Bax's tone-poem for two pianos, *Moy Mell* (1917), which was dedicated to 'Miss Irene Scharrer and Miss Myra Hess', who had given the first performance. I was amused to notice that their names in the dedication did not appear in alphabetical order, but in the order of their then public fame.

The autograph has now joined Bax's other works in the British Library.

Tchaikovsky

Though I was only indirectly concerned with this first edition, it must be mentioned here since it contains features that are little known.

In the mid-1950s I received a letter from James Friskin (1886-1967), an old Scotch friend of Harold Samuel who had taught piano ever since 1913 at the Juilliard School of Music in New York. Both had been pupils at the RCM of Edward Dannreuther.

James had recently been asked by Admiral Hubert Dannreuther, Edward's sole surviving son, what he should do about a certain piece of music he had come across while clearing out his father's library. It was a copy of the first edition (first printing) of the two-piano score of Tchaikovsky's First Piano

Concerto, in which his father had inked-in some 140 alterations in the solo part (mainly in the first movement) to improve the effectiveness of the piano-writing. Tchaikovsky was a friend of Dannreuther, and when staying with him at his house in Orme Square in London had been shown these suggestions. He approved of almost all of them, and arranged that these should be included in the second printing of the work, published by Jurgenson of Moscow in 1879.

The score was eventually given by Admiral Dannreuther to the British Library, where its shelf number is now K.11.d.8.(1). The full story is told (with some facsimiles) in J Friskin, 'The Text of Tchaikovsky's B flat minor Concerto', published posthumously in *Music and Letters*, I (1969), pp. 246-51.

Compositions by HF

Finally I should add some notes about my own autographs. Works written during student days were destroyed in about 1929. Besides the usual piano pieces and songs they included a Sonata for Violin and Piano (1925), which was played at a students' concert at the RCM; a Mass for unaccompanied voices (1926), unperformed; and a *Short Symphony* (1929), played at an RCM Patron's Fund concert and by the Belfast BBC. The only surviving RCM works are a) an unpublished song, *O my deir hert, young Jesus sweit* (1926), written for the birthday of my friend J M de Navarro, in whose effects it turned up after his death in 1979 (now in the Bodleian Library); b) *Five Irish Folk Tunes* for cello and piano (1927), originally published by the Oxford University Press, 1928, but taken over by the Associated Board in 1989; c) A Lyke Wake Dirge (1928), No 2 of *Two Ballads*, Op 1, published by Winthrop Rogers, 1934; and d) the main theme of the second movement of the *Short Symphony* (1929), which was re-used as the opening of the third movement of the Octet, Op 4, published by Hawkes, 1934.

In 1966, some years after I had stopped composition, I gave my surviving autographs to the Bodleian Library, Oxford, with the following explanatory note:

> The suggestion that I should offer to the Bodleian Library any autographs of my own compositions that I still possessed was made by my friend Joy Finzi. She had already given to the Library the autographs of her late husband, Gerald Finzi; and had helped to steer in the same direction those of Sir Hubert Parry (1848-1918) and Robin Milford (1903-59). I therefore felt her suggestion should not be turned down out of hand, even if it did seem rather odd to offer one's own autographs to a library while still alive. Further reflection showed, moreover, that the plan might have some practical advantages, not least that it would provide more space on my own over-crowded shelves. Thus the offer came to be made and accepted.

The autographs comprise two groups: a) those of works that, with one exception (the ballet *Chauntecleer*, Op 11, withdrawn), have been published; and b) a series of 14 bound working Notebooks. The latter require some explanation. From 1925, when I was 17 years old, I formed the habit of using gatherings of MS paper for all my rough work: that is, for stray notes as well as for work in hand. When a composition, or a convenient part of one, was completed, the relevant sheets were bound in chronological order as a volume. Hence each Notebook tends to be centred on one particular work, besides containing notes for others, both finished and unfinished ... The series of Notebooks is indexed, so the growth of any particular work can easily be followed ...

Every composer must find his own way of working, and can waste endless time until he does so. When searching for the way that suited me best, I often wished that I could study the methods of others; but as Beethoven was the only composer whose sketches have survived in any quantity, I could find nobody less intimidating to provide an example. This lack, coupled with an over-tidy habit of mind, gave me the idea of binding up the Notebooks. However little intrinsic value they possess, it will have been worth keeping them if they help to persuade other composers not to destroy their working notes.

Autographs that have not survived are: *Five Irish Folk Tunes* (1927) for cello and piano; Octet, Op 4; *Three Sketches,* Op 14, for flute and piano; and *Five Irish Folksongs,* Op 17, for voice and piano.

Duplicate autographs in the British Library are: Partita, Op 5b, for two pianos; Sonata in F minor, Op 8, for piano; Sonata No 2, Op 10, for violin and piano; and *Amore Langueo,* Op 18, vocal score.

Autographs in other libraries are: *Lovely Armoy* (1954) for unaccompanied SATB (BBC commission), BBC Music Reference Library. *The Dream of the Rood*, Op 19, pencil and ink full score, Fitzwilliam Museum, Cambridge. Nos 3, 2 and 5 of *Five Irish Folk Tunes,* arr for small orchestra, full score; and Nos 2 and 4 of *Four Diversions,* arr for two pianos; both in the BBC Music Library, Belfast.

The system of numbering the works should be explained. In the early 1930s Gerald Finzi and I both felt it would be pretentious to put opus numbers on our published works; nevertheless it was convenient to have some way of identifying them. I suggested it would be sufficient to add a small group of numbers after the final bar of a work, for example, IV (1933), in which the Roman figure would indicate the opus number, and the bracketed numerals the year(s) in which the work was written. Both of us followed this plan; but Gerald's numbering is not always chronological, whereas mine is.

Recordings

Recordings of Howard Ferguson's music available on CD, August 1997:

Orchestral music

Concerto for Piano and Strings, Op 12 (1950-51).
   H Shelley, CLS, R Hickox (r 1986) *Concert*. (EMI) CDM7 64738-2.
Overture for an Occasion, Op 16 (1952-53).
   LSO, R Hickox *Concert*. (CHAN) CHAN 9082
Partita, Op 5a (1935-36)
   LSO, R Hickox *Concert*. (CHAN) CHAN 9082

Chamber music

Octet – cl, bn, hn, stg qt and db, Op 4 (1933)
   Acht Ens (r 1994) *Françaix: Octet* (THOR) CTH 2249
   P Juler, D Brain, C James, J E Merrett, Griller Qt (r 1943) *Concert*
      (DUTT) CDAX 8014
Four Short Pieces – clarinet/viola and piano, Op 6 (1932-36)
   1. Prelude; 2. Scherzo; 3. Pastoral; 4. Burlesque.
   J Hilton, C Benson (r 1994) *Concert* (CHAN) CHAN 9316
   E Jóhannesson, P Jenkins *Concert* (CHAN) CHAN 9079
Three Sketches – flute/treble recorder and piano, Op 14 (1951)
   D Butt, C Benson (r 1994) *Concert* (CHAN) CHAN 9316
Sonata for Violin and Piano No 1, Op 2 (1931)
   L Mordkovitch, C Benson (r 1994) *Concert* (CHAN) CHAN 9316
   J Heifetz, L Steuber *Concert* (RCA) GD 87872
   J Heifetz, L Steuber (r 1966) *Concert* (RCA) 09026 61778-2(43)
Sonata for Violin and Piano No 2, Op 10 (1946)
   F Hunt, U Hunt *Concert* (CNTI) CCD 1051
   L Mordkovitch, C Benson (r 1994) *Concert* (CHAN) CHAN 9316
   L Chilingirian, C Benson *Concert* (HYPE) CDA 66192

Instrumental music

Piano Sonata in F minor, Op 8 (1938-40)
   M Hess (r 1942) *Concert* (BIDD) LHW 025

Vocal and choral music

Amore langueo – tenor, chorus and orchestra, Op 18 (1955-56) (Wds 15th cent)
   M Hill, LSC, CLS, R Hickox (r 1986) *Concert* (HYPE) CDA 66192
Two Ballads – baritone and orchestra, Op 1 (1928-32) (Wds mediaeval anon)
   1. The Twa Corbies; 2. A Lyke Wake Dirge.
   B Rayner Cook, LSC, LSO, R Hickox *Concert* (CHAN) CHAN 9082

Discovery – song cycle: voice and piano, Op 13 (1951) (Wds D Welch)
   1. The Freedom of the City; 2. Babylon; 3. Jane Allen; 4. Discovery;
     5. Dreams melting
   J M Ainsley, C Benson (r 1994) *Concert*   (CHAN) CHAN 9316
   K Ferrier, E Lush (bp 1953) *Concert*   (LOND) 430 061-2LM
                                          (DECC) 430 472-2DM

The Dream of the Rood – S/T, ch and orch, Op 19 (1958-59)
   (Wds, anon Anglo-Saxon)
   Anne Dawson, LSC, LSO, R Hickox *Concert*   (CHAN) CHAN 9082

Five Irish Folk Songs – voice and piano, Op 17 (1954) (Wds anon)
   1. The Apron of Flowers; 2. I'm from over the Mountains; 3. Calen-O;
     4. The Swan; 5. My Grandfather Died.
   S Burgess, C Benson (r 1994) *Concert*   (CHAN) CHAN 9316

Love and Reason – voice and piano
   R Schneider-Waterberg, C Benson (r 1994) *Concert* (CHAN) CHAN 9316

Three Mediaeval Carols – voice and piano, Op 3 (1932-33)
   J M Ainsley, C Benson (r 1994) *Concert*   (CHAN) CHAN 9316

* * *

A number of other recordings have been deleted recently
but copies may still be found in shops.

Index

Allen, Sir Hugh, 13, 18, 24
Ashmansworth, the gardener's cottage, **42-45**

Barton Road, No 51, 88-89, **90-96**
Bass, Emmie, 33, 42
Bax, Sir Arnold: autograph, 101
BBC in wartime, 52
Bechstein, the Upright: at the O'Sullivans', 10; at Clarendon Road, 23; at East Heath Road, 33; at Wildwood Road, 46, 50; fire at Wildwood Road, 86
Belfast, musical life, 7-8
Bennett, Richard Rodney, 63-64
Bliss, Sir Arthur and Lady, 32, 34
Bloch, Ernst, 74
Boosey & Hawkes Ltd, 13, 35, 51
Boston, Lucy, 90-91
Boult, Sir Adrian, 11, 13, 28, 35; soothes Toscanini, 43
Bridge, Frank, 9, 19
Britten, Benjamin, 36-37
Bradshaw, Susan, 63
Brown, Jacques de Froiard, 71-72
Burnett, Winifred, 9
Butt, Richard, 64
Butterworth, George: autograph, 100

Cabell, Hartwell and Louise, 21, 26
California, 12, 73-74
Cardew, Cornelius, 63-64
CEMA, 50, 66
Clark, Sir Kenneth, 55, 57, 61
Cobbe, Hugh, 71-72, 91
Composition, 11, 23, 25-26; *Five Irish Folktunes* (cello), 27-28, 102-103; *Two Ballads*, Op 1, 28, 102; First Violin Sonata, Op 2, 35; *Three Mediaeval Carols*, Op 3, 35; Octet, Op 4, 34-35; Partita, Op 5, 35; Four Short Pieces, Op 6, 35; *Four Diversions*, Op 7, 39, 48, 66; Piano Sonata, Op 8, 42, 49; Five Bagatelles, Op 9, 54-55; Second Violin Sonata, Op 10, 63; *Chauntecleer* ballet, Op 11 (withdrawn), 65; Piano Concerto, Op 12, 65; *Discovery* songs, Op 13, 65; *Three Sketches* (flute), Op 14, 103; *Overture for an Occasion*, Op 16, 66; *Five Irish Folk Songs* (vocal), Op 17, 66; *Amore Langueo*, Op 18, 79-80; *The Dream of the Rood*, 79-80; *Love and Reason* (song), 94-95; *Lovely Armoy* (SATB), 103
Courtauld Trust, 55-56
Creek, Phyllis, 72, 86, 89
Cripps, Sir Stafford and Lady, 54
Cromwell, Anne, *Virginal Book*, 87
Cunningham, Betty, comes to Clarendon Road, 23; illness at East Heath Road, 34; at Willoughby Road, 40; at Ashmansworth, 42; at Wildwood Road, 46, 50, 53; nurses Pu, 67; death, 67-68
Cunningham, May, nanny to HF, 8; leaves Ferguson household, 11; at Inglis Road, 12; housekeeper at Clarendon Road, 23; in New York, 25; to East Heath Road, 34, to Willoughby Road, 40; to Ashmansworth, 42; to Wildwood Road, 46, 50; death, 67

Dahlstrom, Helen and Alton, 74-75
Dart, Thurston, 52, 76
Davie, Cedric Thorpe, 36
Davis, Beryl, 58, 59
Dederich, Hilda, 68-69
Du Pré, Jacqueline, plays at Broadway, 68

East Heath Road, No 8, **33-40**
Editing, 75-77; Schubert, 77-79; *Ann Cromwell's Virginal Book*, 87
Elliott, Stuart D, 36, 65, 81; death, 92
Elgar, Sir Edward: autograph, 97
Elkus, Elizabeth and Albert, 74
Ensemble Players, The, 33-34
Entertaining Solo, 33-34

Ferguson, Edith (niece), 71
Ferguson family, 7
Ferguson, Frances (mother), 7, 40
Ferguson, Howard: childhood, 7; goes to London, 10; sees *Parsifal*, 10; first interest in composition, 11; at Westminster School, 11; at Inglis Road, 12; leaves Westminster, enters RCM, 13; composition scholarship, 24; first and second engagements, 24-25; meets Gerald Finzi, 29; Strauss concert, 29; in New York, 25-27; to Capel, Surrey, 27; leaves RCM, 27; GF's TB, 31; Joy Finzi's head of HF, 31; 8 East Heath Road, **33-40**; learns clarinet, 35; learns German, 36; plays film music, 37; edits Navarro's poems, 39; Mediterranean cruise, 40; Ashmansworth, **42-45**; London Music Festival, 42-43; trip to Germany and Austria, 43-44; car breakdown, 44; returns to Ashmansworth, 44; finds 106 Wildwood Road, 45; Wildwood Road, **46-56**; ghost?, 46-47; friendship with Myra Hess, 48; duo with Isolde Menges, 48; West of Ireland, 49; war, 49; National Gallery Concerts, 49; meets Denis Matthews, 50-51; meets Yfrah Neaman, 51; meets Tim Scott, 53; enters RAF, 53; fifth anniversary of NG Concerts, 55; booklet on NG Concerts, 55; Courtauld Trust, 55-56; NG Concerts end, 56; teaches at RAM, 63; meets Richard Butt, 64; France and Holland with Yfrah, 64-65; Indian tour, 66; holiday in Italy, 68-69; holiday in Sicily, 69-70; meets Hugh Cobbe in Copenhagen, 71; meets Dr Christopher R Wilson, 72; to USA and Canada, 73-75; editing music, **75-77**; editing Schubert, 77-79; non-Christian, 80; stops composition, 81; Greek holiday with AvW, 84; final visit to South Africa, 84; to Corpus Christi College, Cambridge, 85; fire at Wildwood Road, 86; 19c Cranmer Road, 86; return to Wildwood Road, 87; moved to 51 Barton Road, 88; met Lucy Boston, 90; 70th birthday, 91; coronary, 92; Stuart's death, 92; 80th birthday, 92; CD recordings, 93; met Reiner, 94; to Chartres with R, 95; Schubertiade at Feldkirch, 95; 85th birthday and concert, 95; R leaves Cambridge, 96; Riemenschneider trip, 96; HF's autographs, 102-103
Ferguson, Stanley (father), 7, 40
Finzi, Gerald, **29-32**; uncertainty in works, 30; gets TB, 31; meets and marries Joy, 31; at Downshire Hill, 31; at Aldbourne, 31-32; Ashmansworth, 32; death, 80-81
Forster, E M, 55

Gilbert, Kenneth, 71-72
Gishford, Anthony, 13
Grieg, Edvard: first edition, 101
Griller Quartet, 35, 52, 56
Gurney, Ivor: autographs, 100-101

Harland, Peter, 32
Hess, Myra, 38, 48, 49, 53; National Gallery Concerts, **57-62**; Cripps at No 48, 54; returns to Holland, 61; plays HF's concerto, 65; holiday in Sicily, 69-70; holiday in Paris, 70; death, 70
Hoffnung, Gerard, 47-48
Hogwood, Christopher, 90
Hokanson, Randolph, 40, 74

Ibbs & Tillett Ltd, 33, 59
Inglis Road, No 12, 12

James, Ivor, 15, 27, 37
James, Warwick, 37, 41
Johnson, Mrs Margaret: trip to Germany and Austria, 43-44; death of daughter, 45; gift of Steinway, 50
Jones, Alan, 77, 79
Jones, Geraint, 51
Juler, Pauline, 35, 51

Keyboard Duets, 94
Keyboard Interpretation, 77
Keynes, Dr Geoffrey, 34
Kovasevich, Stephen, 47, 68, 91
Kraft, Hertha, 36

Latham, Tony, 70-71
Lawrence, T E, 38
Luckhurst, Nigel, 64

Mozart, Wolfgang Amadeus: autographs, 97-98
Mannheimer, Frank, 69-70, 74
Matthews, Denis, 50-51, 91
Menges, Isolde, 48
Moore, Mrs Bessie, 9
Morris, R O: at RCM, 13-14, 27; in Philadelphia, 26, 49
Musicians' Benevolent Fund, 58, 62
MacIlwaine, Mrs Jack, 9, 39, 48

National Gallery Concerts, 49, 50-51, 55, 56, **57-62**; programme planning, 59; time-bomb, 60; statistics, 61-62
Navarro, Toty (José Maria) de, 25; poems, 38-39; bombs at Wildwood Road, 53
Neaman, Yfrah, 51, 64-65, 91
New York, 25-27, 73

Oakley, Dr Douglas, 34, 41
O'Sullivan, Biddy, 10, 11; organises Debussy's *Boîte à Joujoux*, 12
O'Sullivan, Mrs Denis, 10, 11; leaves for California, 12

Parry, Sir Hubert: autographs, 99

Rachmaninov, Sergei: Fourth Piano Concerto, 26
Royal Academy of Music, 63-64
Royal College of Music: HF enters, 13; hears opera, 15; HF leaves, 27

Samuel, Harold, 9; gives prize to HF, 9; meets HF's parents, 9; lends HF Bechstein upright, 10; sets up house at 12 Inglis Road, 12, **16-22**; accompanies male alto, 16; enters RCM, 16; first recital, 16; accompanist and teacher, 16; second recital, 17; first Bach Week, 17-18; Tovey and Bach's 48, 18; dislike of harpsichord, 19; Frank Bridge Sonata, 19; memory and nerves, 19-20; compositions, 20; first South African tour, 21; first USA tour, 21; his mother's death, 21; character, 21-22; at Clarendon Road, 23; stay in New York, 25-27; Canadian tour, 40; last South African tour, 40; coronary, 41; death, 41.
Sargent, Malcolm, 14-15
Sawyer, Frederick J, 8, 20
Scharrer, Irene, 38
Schiff, András, 19, 93
Scott, Tim, 53
Schneider-Waterberg, Reiner, 94-96
Schubert, Franz: HF's edition, 77-79; sources, 98
Stanford, Sir Charles: autographs and editions, 98
Steinway 'Model A grand', 50, 88; fire at Wildwood Road, 86, 91
Stratton Quartet, 35

Tanner, Michael, 85
Tchaikovsky, Pyotr Ilyich: first edition, 101-102
Toscanini, Arturo, 26, 43
Tubb, Carrie, 24

Van Wyk, Arnold, 55, 66, **82-84**; returns to South Africa, 83; death, 84; HF edits works, 84; CDs, 84
Vaughan Williams, Ralph: *Hugh the Drover* at RCM, 15; HF studies with RVW at RCM, 27
Violin: homemade, 8-9; violin lessons, 9

Walter, Bruno, 26, 39
Walton, Sir William: first performances, 30, 33; autographs, 99-100
Westminster School: enters, 11; leaves, 12-13
Wildwood Road, No 106: pre-war and war years, **46-56**; post-war years, **63-81**; ghost?, 46-47; fire, 86
Willoughby Road, No 34, 40
Wilson, Christopher R, 72-73; 92
Wood, Sir Henry, 14, 48-49